KREGEL CLASSIC SERMONS SERIES

CLASSIC SERMONS
ON
HOPE

Compiled by
Warren W. Wiersbe

kregel
PUBLICATIONS

Grand Rapids, MI 49501

Classic Sermons on Hope, compiled by Warren W. Wiersbe.

Copyright © 1994 by Kregel Publications. All rights reserved. No part of this book may be reproduced, stored in a retrieval system, or transmitted in any form or by any means—electronic, mechanical, photocopy, recording, or otherwise—without written permission of the publisher, except for brief quotations in printed reviews.

Published by Kregel Publications, a division of Kregel, Inc., P.O. Box 2607, Grand Rapids, MI 49501. Kregel Publications provides trusted, biblical publications for Christian growth and service. Your comments and suggestions are valued.

Cover and Book Design: Alan G. Hartman

Library of Congress Cataloging-in-Publication Data

Classic Sermons on hope / compiled by Warren W. Wiersbe.
    p.   cm.— (Kregel classic sermons series)
    Includes index.
    1. Hope—Religious aspects—Christianity—Sermons.
2. Sermons, English. 3. Sermons, American. I. Wiersbe,
Warren W. II. Series: Kregel classic sermons series.
BV4638.C53   1994   234'.2—dc20   93-41452
                                                                        CIP

ISBN   0-8254-4045-9 (pbk.)

1 2 3 4 5 Printing / Year 98 97 96 95 94

Printed in the United States of America

CONTENTS

LIST OF SCRIPTURE TEXTS

PREFACE

The *KREGEL CLASSIC SERMONS SERIES* is an attempt to assemble and publish meaningful sermons from master preachers about significant themes.

These are *sermons*, not essays or chapters taken from books about themes. Not all of these sermons could be called "great," but all of them are *meaningful*. They apply the truths of the Bible to the needs of the human heart which is something that all effective preaching must do.

While some are better known than others, all of the preachers, whose sermons I have selected, had important ministries and were highly respected in their day. The fact that a sermon is included in this volume does not mean that either the compiler or the publisher agrees with or endorses everything that the man did, preached, or wrote. The sermon is here because it has a valued contribution to make.

These are sermons about *significant* themes. The pulpit is no place to play with trivia. The preacher has thirty minutes in which to help mend broken hearts, change defeated lives, and save lost souls; and one can never accomplish this demanding ministry by distributing homiletical tidbits. In these difficult days, we do not need "clever" pulpiteers who discuss the times; we need dedicated ambassadors who will preach the eternities.

The reading of these sermons can enrich your own spiritual life. The studying of them can enrich your own skills as an interpreter and expounder of God's truth. However God uses these sermons in your own life and ministry, my prayer is that His church around the world will be encouraged and strengthened.

WARREN W. WIERSBE

A Message for Gray Days

Arthur John Gossip (1873–1954) pastored churches in England and Scotland before becoming Professor of Practical Theology at Trinity College, Glasgow. He gave the Warrack Lectures on Preaching in 1925, published under the title *In Christ's Stead*, and he published several books of sermons. He was not a dramatic preacher, but the intensity of his delivery and the depth of his message and character attracted and held the listeners. Perhaps his most famous sermon is "But When Life Tumbles In, What Then?" which he preached the Sunday after his wife suddenly died after what was supposed to be minor surgery.

This message is taken from his book *The Hero in Thy Soul*, published in 1930 by Charles Scribner's Sons, New York.

Arthur John Gossip

1

A MESSAGE FOR GRAY DAYS

> If the vision tarry, wait for it, for it will come: and it will
> not be late (Habakkuk 2:3, *Moffatt*).

THERE, TO BEGIN WITH, is a claim on you and me, a warning
that if we wish to be really helpful to God and our fellows we
must cultivate a certain calm and equanimity of mind, a
certain valor and imperturbability of spirit that believes in
righteousness and the success of its cause much too stout-
heartedly to grow afraid even if things do drag a bit, that
knows God far too well to think of doubting Him even if His
promises seem slow of foot and our dreams lag and the time
grows longer than we hoped.

The function of religious people, so this tired man heard
God saying to his heart in dark and trying days when
there was not much to encourage, what is it? What do I
set them in the world to do? What is it that I ask of them?
Is it not largely this—to keep cool and unfidgety when
other folk are growing flustered about things; to look out
upon this confusing life with steady eyes when those
around them, badly scared, have taken to glancing back
across their shoulders, and there is that ominous feeling
of panic in the air; to trust Me not only when that is easy
and the sun is shining but when there is most need for
faith, yes, and some valor in the offer of it?

Suppose the times are disappointing and disquieting,
that I [God] seem to have forgotten, appear not to care;
that in spite of all your efforts nothing, so you judge, is
happening. Still, don't get nervy and irritable, fussy and
on edge. Don't toss your dream impatiently away as something that evidently can never come to pass in this dusty
workaday world of drab realities. Still hold to it, work
for it, believe in it, expect it. If the vision tarry, wait for
it; grant Me some loyalty and some tenacity of purpose

and some common courage. Give Me that—long enough—
and we win.

It must, surely, be a little daunting to ardent spirits to
note how often in the Scriptures that is God's message to
His people. Age after age, apparently, earnest souls feel
hotly that the world is out of joint, that something must be
done to mend things; yes, and they see what that is and
start up eagerly to set about it, sure that they can put it
through. And, age after age, in a little they are standing
puzzled and daunted and confused with their resolution
oozing from them, tired and dispirited. For do what they
will and can, so little seems to come of it. And it is like that
last wild tumult of a fight in Lyonnesse when even the
king felt, or half felt, that all that he had done and all that
he had tried had been in vain; men fought blindly with
that horrible fog not only in the air but stealing chokingly
into their very souls and fell, too many of them, and as
they fell, "looked up to heaven and only saw the mist."

And, age after age, God has to call to them not to allow
themselves to be tamed and broken, not to grow acquies-
cent in things as they are, not to abandon their audacious
hopes but to keep daring and expectant. If the vision
tarry, wait for it. Hold on a little longer though your very
souls are growing so numbed that they can hardly keep
their grip. Wait, He keeps urging, wait.

The Difficulty of Waiting

That is a very common message to God's people. And
yet to wait can be the hardest thing in the whole world.
"We can do nothing more," the doctor says, "we must just
wait." But that is dreadful. If we could help in any way, it
would not be nearly so hard. But to sit still with empty,
useless, idle hands while that dear life hangs in suspense,
the thing is maddening. Or when an attack was ordered,
much the worst time was those awful moments lined up
in the trench while the officer, his eyes upon his watch,
waited for the appointed second with one's every tense
nerve strained and twittering, with one's mind running
on and on with queerly quick, short, breathless steps till
one could have screamed: "Blow that whistle and let us

get over and be done with it, one way or the other. Better that than this long agony of waiting." Yet God often asks His children to wait.

Not that they are to dawdle about until something turns up or even to stand with their eyes fastened greedily on the horizon. If anything much is to happen for God in our time, then we must do it for Him, must throw in wholeheartedly all that we have into His service, must be eager and zealous over it. That is, indeed, where we too often fail and why, not seldom, things move so exasperatingly slowly. We are listless, apathetic, only half in earnest. And then with cool effrontery, we throw the blame on God. We can't understand, we say loftily, why One who is Almighty does not do far more for this desperate world. Why? answers God. Because you failed Me, because at the pinch, the faith and courage and zeal on which I counted were not there.

But even if we are in deadly earnest, we must add something more to our equipment or inevitably we shall break down under the strain of things before the end. We must be not only enthusiastic and on fire but at the same time cool and patient, working as tirelessly as if this were the one and only time that what we see could ever come to pass and yet not peevish and discouraged if there prove to be delay, doing our duty loyally yet with a quiet and unflurried mind, leaving the times and seasons to God's choosing.

That last is not easy; and the more in earnest that we are, the harder does it grow. Kingsley, quoting the Scripture, "He that believeth will not make haste," flamed out in his hot way: "And yet I think that he that believeth can do nothing except haste; look at the world!" And indeed, it is extraordinarily difficult not at times to lose patience with God, not to be filled with what Hilary of Poitiers called "an irreligious solicitude for Him," not to have the feeling that He is not managing well and that surely He might do vastly more if only He would really try, not to keep running on ahead of Him like an excited child and back time after time to tug impatiently at His hand, seeking to hasten His slow steps and always crying "Hurry, hurry," not to grow fussy and hot and out of breath, even to sulk, declaring with a whimper like a petted child that we won't play unless our hands are to haul down the enemies' flag, and our eyes are allowed to see the final wild exhilarating rush of victory sweeping all before it.

But it is not that God is slow or less in earnest than we are. Ah! who of us can doubt Him now? For who of us has gone the length of Calvary? Shall we compare our futile little bits of earnestness with that? It is that human nature is much more crabbed and stubborn than we with our superficial diagnoses realize and that evils have far deeper roots than we imagine and won't come up, as we hope, with one sharp tug and that the road to our ideals is much longer than it looks when we set out on it. Don't you remember Masefield?

> Not for us are content, and quiet, and peace of mind,
> For we go seeking a city that we shall never find.
> Only the road, and the dawn, the sun, and the wind, and
>   the rain,
> And the watch fire under the stars, and sleep, and the
>   road again.
> We travel the dusty road, till the light of the day is dim,
> And the sunset shows us spires, away on the world's rim.

God's Dare to Those Who Wait

Yes, says God, this may prove a longer and much slower business than you estimate. I have had gallant servants who gave Me their whole life, everything that they had, and yet they died in faith, not having received the promises but with their faces still turned doggedly in their direction, and still certain they would come. And if you have been set down in a difficult day, can you too give Me a like steadfastness, dare you too work on unafraid without much to encourage you but still infecting those around you with your unconcerned and quiet faith, a faith that never dreams of doubting Me?

> Love, love that once for me did agonize
> Will conquer all things to itself. If late

Or soon it be, I ask not, nor advise.
But, since my God is waiting, I can wait.

Faith, hope, love, these are great gifts. And yet not faith, not hope, not love, not even all of them together will of themselves bring you through with honor. For that, something even more is needed. Remember, says St. Anthony, of all the virtues, perseverance alone wins the crown. Have you the cold, dour courage that checked and beaten back can set its teeth and hold its ground and have never a thought of giving way? For that is often what I need in those who would serve Me, says God. If it tarry, wait.

And so in our own lives. "We all thought," said Baxter, speaking of the Civil War, "that one battle would end it, but we were all very much mistaken." And so, I suppose, most of us expected that our spiritual life would move on in some ways much faster than it has. We knew we had certain temptations, but we were going to knock them on the head and so an end of that; yet perhaps some of them visit us to this day with the old hateful cunning. We were aware that we were prone to this and that humbling sin and weakness. But Christ would break them for us. Yet, perhaps, some of them still stubbornly persist.

We saw the glory of life as Christ led it, and our hearts ran out to that eagerly. But it has proved more difficult to weave our matted character into His likeness than we thought! We too have need of that prayer that Paul tells us he kept urging on behalf of certain of his friends that our "faith may become a thing of power." For as things are, it seems sometimes curiously ineffective, does it not, in our particular case? Even a gram of it will remove mountains, we are promised; and indeed we too, like Bunyan, have seen men tumbling about the hills with it, seen natures that seemed set rebuilt from their foundations upon a new plan, and men and women who had sunk very low, transformed and glorified beyond belief. But our own records somehow seem far tamer and much duller.

Ananda, Buddha's favorite disciple, saw comrade after comrade reach Nirvana. Yet though he loved as few among them loved, year after year slipped past, and for him it seemed far away as ever, and the marvelous chance for all his longing in his case would not work out. And we too do have faith in Christ, and we too do look toward Him. And yet, and yet our faith is not the thing of power it manifestly is for many another. Yes, says God, sometimes it is very slow. But don't you throw away your hope, hold to it, wait.

And to teach you that hard lesson, look at Jesus Christ who, though plans broke and friends deserted Him and God Himself seemed strangely callous to it all, held on unflinchingly and waited though the crowds were plainly leaving Him and a huge storm was obviously blowing up and it did break on Him at last and in the end they nailed Him to a cross; waited even then, unafraid even there, for the vision that had tarried, ah! how long, still certain it would come! "The patience of Christ," says Paul, laying his hand on what most struck him in the Master; may God direct your fretful hearts to that. If you would face life bravely and big-heartedly, keep close to Him. For to a certainty you too will need to learn to wait if you would really serve God and the Cause and not break down at times into a whimper of disloyalty nor be guilty of an insolence so gross that it can seek to hector God, to instruct the All-Wise and that not without a certain peremptory sharpness at His dullness. Steady, there! Steady! Wait!

A Promise from God

But further, there is here a promise that may well rally the most dispirited. "It will come," so God tells us; you can count upon that; "it will come." It is no futile fancy, no mere dream, maddeningly impossible as when out in the trenches, sick of the mud and the shelling and the war, you sat and dreamed such vivid dreams of home that for the moment you seemed there among your own again. And with that someone spoke or jostled you, and it was gone, was far away as ever, and with a jolt you were back in the mud and the shelling and the war. Blessedly, it is not like that. "All we have hoped or dreamed of good," says our brave poet, "shall exist, not its semblance but itself. The hard that proved too hard, the heroic for earth too high," will all come true—will surely all come true. I promise it, says God. If you will play your part, you can depend on Me. It is upon the road though you see nothing; the seed is living and is springing up, and it will flower. Winter turns spring, and spring grows summer every year.

Is it not well to be reminded of that sometimes? For there is much in history to daunt and not a little to make one cynical. Here are we, for example, all agog over the League of Nations. And yet experts, who presumably are cognizant of the facts, assure us that since the days of Henry VI this is the twenty-sixth attempt to eliminate war by some kind of international agreement that has been started with high hopes! Twenty-five times others have seen the vision that we see; twenty-five times have they pursued it eagerly; five-and-twenty times it dimmed, flickered, and went out. And now once more we are out on the old quest that has for so long baffled so many others. Yes, say many, it is demonstrably useless and a wild foolish chase of what is unattainable that can only leave us hot and breathless and ruffled in our tempers and depressed.

But no, says the prophet, "it will come." The Reformation too before Luther's day was broken more than twenty times. Again and again the flames were fiercely stamped out, quenched in blood. Yet it did come at last. Over and over, the embers that seemed cold grew red again until there dawned a day when the winds of God were abroad in the earth; almost suddenly, these fanned the uncertain flames into a roaring fire that rushed, free and untamable, across the world.

No effort in the cause of truth is ever useless even when, mathematically, the result appears to be exactly nothing except withered hopes and wasted energies. Each new attempt revives the idea in men's minds, keeps it alive, sends some remembrance of it down the ages, hands on a high tradition.

It is like those sham attacks out at the front that seemed to end only in cruel ruin and inexplicable bungling with men's lives. I have spoken to a Divisional Commander before whom as a rule one walked in fear and trembling, forgetful of all seemliness, and swept away by a hot anger. "Look at my boys," I cried, standing there among the ghastly wreckage, "look at my boys!" And the man answered with tears in his eyes, "God knows, padre, I did not wish this. But because of this, the enemy's line is broken miles away!" And all these efforts after some great truth or high ideal that were balked or driven back were not for nothing. Always we can be absolutely sure, even if we are disappointed and our eyes see only tired men who have given much and gained nothing at all, that because of this somewhere down the coming years the enemy's line will break.

Indeed, history makes heartening reading. There were once horrible diseases rampant in our land, leprosy for one of them. It was not only Edinburgh that had its Liberton, its lepers' town; many a country church still shows the old lepers' window through which these poor outcasts won some share in that from which they were excluded. Everywhere, here and there, one came upon that horror on maimed broken lives shut in to a huge, ugly, awful misery. And it is gone, gone utterly, like a hideous nightmare from which one awakes and in a little while forgets about it. And moral evils that had seemed engrained in the make-up of things have vanished no less thoroughly. For years, for centuries, legal hearts strained toward these achievements and they seemed no nearer; and yet they are here. "It will come," says the prophet; in God's name I promise it, if only we keep valiant.

True, at the best it is not easy to unravel the tangled web of things. The enemy rallies so surprisingly and has such uncanny skill in snatching a new victory out of crushing defeat. I once lived in a little town which had in older days a most unenviable reputation for consumption. The doctors started a crusade; slowly, surely, at a gradually quickening pace, the thing died down; but as it died, almost with equal steps cancer increased, and the last state appeared to be more evil than the first.

Morley gives a somber reading of not a little of our confident activities. We see some evil, evolve a solution of it, push that through with long effort and sacrifice; straightway the new situation may engender some new evil which may prove even more intractable and difficult to meet! We have won liberty, for instance, and what are we doing with that glorious thing now it is ours? Filling the land with raucous cries, pushing and jostling one another in a wild, selfish stampede, each after our class interest or personal gain!

Aye, it is slow and often disappointing! And yet would you have us serfs again? What can be done except give us our liberty and let us learn to use it seemingly in time. Believe me, said the Romanist in Reformation days, if your mad scheme grows real, there can be nothing but disaster. For the people are not fit for the responsibilities and powers you are conceding them. Your churches will be empty, your Scriptures mishandled, your land filled with half-baked theories of half-ignorant minds; you need authority to guide and to control, and you are wantonly destroying it. Well, the churches are half empty, the Bible is not reverenced as once it was, and an amazing mass of confident nonsense is being talked with truculent assurance by people with small right to an opinion who do not even know how ignorant they are!

Certainty Through Difficulty

There may be difficult times before us, granted, but would you have us back at the old subservience again? Surely a child must be set down upon its feet if it is ever to learn to walk! That must cause many a stumble, may mean many a sore fall; but only so can it develop the powers it is meant to use. And though much may seem irritating, vexing, disappointing, still if we keep our faces toward the light and push on as we can, it will come in the end. For it is not for nothing that the popular mode of thought sees an advance, a progress, a slow, painful evolution in the trend of things. There may be, there is, many a slip back and fall and blunder. Still, "it does move." And "it will come."

In our time? That may be. But certainly if we are faithful, some time. And is it not enough for us to play our part and let who may be destined for that reap the glory? Even Jesus Christ saw little. Once by a glorious feat of heroism the battalion saved the line. And three days later as the tired boys lay about a barn speaking with small voices almost inaudible through weariness, the papers came. By an inexplicable slip the credit of the feat was given to a battalion who were miles away, and ours was never mentioned. There fell a somber silence, and the Colonel's face flushed red. And then his head went up. "Gentlemen," he said proudly, "what does it matter who gets the credit of it? We know we did it." Enough for us that we be faithful. It will come.

And in our own lives also. Perhaps you are depressed, dissatisfied with things, haunted by an uneasy feeling that after all your faith and efforts you are painfully little changed from your original uncouthness, that not enough is coming of it, that if the real Christ were really in your life surely there would be greatly more to show. Look, your heart cries, how it was in His time! How everywhere He went there were extraordinary happenings, things glorious, undeniable, and there for all to see. But I, what can I show?

Toward the end, Marcus Dods, whom Robertson Nicoll called the most Christlike man he had ever seen, felt that about himself with gnawing acuteness but used to fortify his heart with a chemical metaphor. Into a liquid is dropped one drop or a second, and there is no result—another, and another, many others, one by one, apparently in vain—and then one more, precisely like the rest, and all of a sudden not as the outcome of that last alone but as the culmination of the whole seemingly useless process, everything is changed! And day by day doggedly we pray and hope and toil and believe. And what is there to show for it? Not much, to outward seeming, it may be. And yet is far more going on than our eyes see? And one day may one other prayer, one other ordinary act of common faith, one more looking toward Jesus Christ bring the long process to its culmination, and we waken satisfied because in His likeness—at last!

Sudden or slow, dramatic or invisible, "it will come"—it will come! After all, says Samuel Rutherford, the end is sure: a long, steep road, a tired, footsore traveler, and a warm welcome home, that is the worst that there can be.

For, says the prophet, "it will not be late." That is the fear that often haunts us. It is too late, men say of the old land. She has heeled so far over in the gale that she can't right herself—is doomed! Such talk, one fancies, is the way to bring disaster on us. If only we will pay our taxes cheerfully and face a more pinched way of life than we would naturally choose and think not only of our own but other people's interests, please God, we will come through it yet.

But that "too late" is a grievous reality, a grim and fearsome fact of life. The other day I was taking the service at a baby's funeral and, among others, read the passage, "There shall be no more death, neither sorrow, nor crying for the former things are passed away." And then I looked across at the mother, wondering if that was helping her or only wounding her poor heart? It is a bonnie promise! Ah, if only it had come in time! But in one sense, at least, its fulfillment is too late for her. Her boy is dead!

Often that is what we feel about ourselves. Once, not a doubt, it might have been. We might have really closed with Christ and really taken what He offers us. But now our character is fixed, our habits are settled, the channels cut in which the rivers must run to the end. It is too late. And there is dreadful truth in that.

"Sleep on now," said the Master sadly, the glorious office He had offered His friends left unaccepted and refused; sleep on, it does not matter now. The chance is lost, the opportunity is past, sleep on! The boy who in the afternoon repented of his surliness and went, could only offer a few hours of work at most, not a full day. That had become impossible forever.

Every failure in a way is irremediable. Always our record must be to the end by that amount less than it might and should and could have been. The crooked can't be made straight; what is lacking can't be numbered. And you and I look wistfully across at Christ and then sadly enough at what we are. That is what I might have been, and this is what I am; that is what I was offered, and this is what I chose! Fool that I was, but now—it is too late.

But the whole point of the Gospel is that in one glorious way, it is not yet too late for anyone. If you have not seen that in Christ, have you seen Christ at all? Always He faced the poorest, the most soiled and tangled life, with the sure confidence that even yet it could be righted; yes, and He would do it now. And how often and how strangely He was justified in cases that looked just impossible! Aye, and why should He not be so in you and me? It is to us, remember, to plain ordinary folk like you and me that He gives His bewildering promises; it is on us He makes His staggering claims; it is for us He prays those astounding prayers of His with their tremendous hopes! To that, then, He feels even yet we can attain.

> Death closes all: but something e'er the end,
> Some work of noble note, may yet be done.
> The lights begin to twinkle from the rocks,
> The long day wanes: the slow moon climbs: the deep
> Moans round with many voices. Come, my friends,
> 'Tis not too late, to seek a newer world.

No, it is not too late, even for you and me, to throw ourselves on Jesus Christ, really to take, really to use, that strange power that He offers and so really grow— yes, you and I—into His blessed likeness, not too late for God's dream of us to come really true.

Up! up! and back into the thick of things with steady hearts and quiet eyes. And, even "if it tarry, wait for it, for it will come: and it will not be late."

NOTES

The Optimism of Jesus

John Daniel Jones (1865–1942) served for 40 years at
the Richmond Hill Congregational Church in
Bournemouth, England, where he ministered the Word
with a remarkable consistency of quality and effectiveness,
as his many volumes of published sermons attest. A leader
in his denomination, he gave himself to church extension
(he helped to start 30 new churches), assistance to needier
congregations, and increased salaries for the clergy. He
spoke at D. L.. Moody's Northfield Conference in 1919.

This sermon is from his book, *The Gospel of Grace.*

John Daniel Jones

2

THE OPTIMISM OF JESUS

Jesus looked upon him and said, Thou art Simon, the son of John: thou shalt be called Cephas (which is by interpretation, Peter) (John 1:42).

I AM NOT going to discuss in any detail the beautiful story of the calling of the first disciples—full of instruction and inspiration though it is. My interest just now is not in the men who were called but in the Man who called them, not in Andrew or John or James or even in Peter, but in Jesus. This verse from one point of view is a key to the character of Peter. It epitomizes his life story. For that is exactly what his life story is—it is the story of the evolution of Peter, the man of rock, out of the impulsive and unstable Simon. But this verse does more than give us an insight into Peter's character; it is also a revelation of what I may term the *method of Jesus*, and it is from that point of view I want just now to look at it.

The Method of Jesus

Now when I speak of the *method of Jesus*, I mean the method by which He sought to fulfill His mission and do the work which His Father had given Him to do. What was that mission? It was a mission of redemption. This was how Jesus Himself described it at the very beginning of His career. "The Spirit of the Lord is upon Me, because He hath anointed Me to preach good tidings to the poor: He hath sent Me to proclaim release to the captives and recovering of sight to the blind, to set at liberty them that are bruised, to proclaim the acceptable year of the Lord." Or as He put it at a later stage of His career in still simpler and plainer words, "The Son of Man came to seek and to save that which was lost."

Now this mission which our Lord set before Himself

was one which He also gloriously accomplished. Christ not only *came* to redeem, but He actually *did* redeem. He saved some who seemed utterly beyond hope of saving. He raked the gutter for His saints. Zacchæus and the woman who was a sinner and the dying thief are shining illustrations of a redeeming power to which no task of redemption was impossible.

Now whenever we hear or read of any remarkable achievement, we want to know how it is done. When the seemingly impossible is accomplished beneath our eyes, we want to know what is the secret. And so when we read of Jesus Christ's redeeming power, when we hear of Him succeeding in the most desperate of cases, when we see Him transforming the swindler and the harlot not simply into respectable members of society but into veritable saints of God, we want to know how He did it. What was His secret? How was it He was able to do things in the way of redemption that no one before or since has been able to equal or even to approach? What is there about the *method* of Jesus to account for it all?

Let me not be misunderstood, however. In talking about the *method* of Jesus I do not want to suggest for one moment that the difference between Him and other teachers and reformers was merely one of *method*. I do not want it to be supposed that the secret of Christ's redeeming power is to be found in some mere mechanical trick or happy manner. The difference between Christ and everyone else in the world's history is not one of *mechanics*; it is, shall I say, one of *dynamics*. It is not one of *method* but of *power*. Christ was able to redeem men of whom every human agency had despaired, not because of some happy knack, but because He possessed a power that no human agency possessed.

In the last resort, Christ's redeeming power springs from His everlasting Deity. At the same time, comparing Christ with other would-be redeemers—quite apart from His Deity—there are certain qualities about Him, certain methods which He adopted which, once we grasp their significance, help us to understand how it was He succeeded where every human agency had failed.

Christ's Optimism

The particular point in the "method" of Jesus that I want to emphasize is His "optimism." Christ in His attitude toward men and in His opinion of them was a radiant and invincible optimist. He was this in spite of the fact that something was sorely and sadly amiss with man. It was apparent to the most casual observer that the whole head was sick and the whole heart faint—that he was full of wounds and bruises and festering sores.

Palestine in Christ's days had its problem in the shape of that great outcast class known as "publicans and sinners," just as we have our problem today in the mean street and the city slum and the submerged tenth. And in addition to the abject misery and wretchedness of the outcast class, there were the miseries and ills of the personal life, the weariness and the unrest and the sin of the individual soul.

Matthew Arnold, I think it is, says of Goethe that he was able to lay his finger with unerring accuracy upon the real seat of human mischief and ill and say, "Thou ailest here and here." It is not Goethe alone who has been able to do that. Many have been able to do it. Jesus Himself was able to do it. If you want an illustration of the way in which Jesus could lay His finger on the very spot, read the story of the sick of the palsy. Those four friends of his thought all the mischief was physical. It was just a matter of those paralyzed and helpless limbs, they imagined.

Jesus knew better. He knew the real problem was deeper down. He put His finger on the very spot when with His first word He said, "Son, thy sins are forgiven thee." Yes, Jesus knew better than anyone else all about man's sickness and disease. The difference between other thinkers and teachers and Jesus is this—that while they saw the disease and *despaired*, He saw the disease and *hoped*. That is the splendid characteristic of Jesus—His superb and almost audacious optimism. He despaired of none; He knew nothing of hopeless classes.

He had hope even for the "devil's castaways," as George Whitefield would say. That is one of our Lord's characteristics that lies on the very surface of the Gospel story. Perhaps the one feature of our Lord's conduct that aroused most comment and controversy was His friendship for "publicans and sinners." But that friendship was at once the outcome and the proof of His glorious optimism.

The religious people of Palestine—the Pharisees and scribes—had given up these people as hopeless; they had abandoned them to their fate. "This people," they said, "that knoweth not the law is accursed." But Jesus deliberately cultivated their friendship; He became the "friend of publicans and sinners" not simply because He believed they were *worth* saving, but also because He believed with all His heart that they *could* be saved. And this hope was one that did not put Him to shame, for out of these abandoned and outcast classes, He gathered some of the most faithful and loyal of His disciples.

And our Lord's optimism, let me add, was not a blind and ignorant optimism. It was an intelligent optimism; it was a reasoned optimism; it was an optimism that was optimistic in the light of full and perfect knowledge. There is an ignorant and shallow optimism, an optimism that turns a blind eye to all hard and bitter and unpleasant facts and then prates about everything being as it should be in the best possible of worlds. But Christ's optimism was not of that sort. All the Evangelists bear witness to His wondrous powers of insight. "He needed not," says John, "that any one should bear witness concerning man, for He Himself knew what was in man." He could read men through and through.

The gospels often refer to the "gaze" of Jesus Christ, and the word they use suggests a look that takes in not simply a man's outward characteristics but pierces right into his heart and soul. Jesus knew man in and out. Nothing was hidden or secret from Him. All man's inner and unseen sin and shame lay naked and open to His searching glance. "This man," said Simon in his patronizing way, "if He had been a prophet, would have known who and what manner of woman this is that toucheth Him, for she is a sinner."

Would have known? Jesus knew better than Simon or

any Pharisee in the land. No one knew so much about human sin as Jesus; no one had such clear vision of it; no one had such a realization of the horror of it. And yet, knowing all, He hoped. Though He could read every heart like a book, He *hoped*. And yet why should I say "*though* He could read"? I ought rather to say, "*because* He could read."

Jesus was optimistic not *in spite of* knowing all but *because* He knew all. He *hoped* just because His eye could search into the deepest recesses of the soul. Simon and other Pharisees like him saw the superficial facts—the sin, the vice, the shame—and they despaired. Jesus saw deeper and further, and *hoped*. I have read somewhere of one of the great Italian sculptors that one day, seeing a rough and misshapen block of marble which had been cast aside as worthless and useless, he was seized as with a kind of Divine fury and began to use his hammer and chisel, and as he made the chips of marble fly he said to those who watched him, "Let me unloose the angel." With his quick artist's eye he had seen the angel in that rough, misshapen, and outcast block.

In much the same way, in the world's waste and outcast material, Jesus saw what no one else saw. He saw the hidden and buried angel. Behind and beneath the sin and folly and shame He saw glorious potencies and possibilities. Down in the human heart, overlaid perhaps by wickedness and vice, He saw feelings lay buried which grace could restore. He saw the hidden and sleeping angel in the rough fishermen of Galilee, in Zacchæus and Mary, in all sorts of publicans and sinners, and He became their friend just because He believed the angel in every man could be unloosed. Christ's optimism was an optimism in view of all the facts. The Person who knew man best was the One who hoped for him the most.

The Redeeming Power of Hope

Now I want to ask you to notice that Christ's optimism was in part the *secret of His redeeming power*. He was able to redeem men just because He was full of radiant hope for them. We know something of the saving power of hope in everyday life. Take the matter of physical illness for illustration. We scoff sometimes at faith-healing, but as in the case of nearly every belief that takes possession of the human mind, there is a modicum of truth at the heart of it. Indeed, it is just the solid bit of truth there is in it that has given Christian Science its immense vogue in America. And the truth in it is this—that soul and body act and interact and that physical health is largely affected by spiritual conditions.

The first condition of recovery is *hope* in its possibility, belief on the part of the patient that he *can* recover. A hopeless patient is a doomed patient; so the first thing the wise doctor does is to try to kindle hope; hope is as necessary to the cure as medicine. Now it is much like that with the more dread and terrible diseases that afflict the soul. Hope plays a large part in moral and spiritual recovery. Indeed, the Apostle waxes very bold and says, "We are saved by *hope*."

Notice that. "Saved by *hope*." The first condition of salvation is a hope and belief that we can be saved! We know that from our own experience. If we want to help a man who is down, how do we set about it? We try to kindle hope in him; we talk of the possibilities still before him. We can never help a man if we despair of him. Despair damns men. Despair drives men deeper into sin and shame. Now, Pharisees and scribes could do nothing toward the redemption of "publicans and sinners" because they despaired of them. Indeed, I will go further and say that the attitude of Pharisees and scribes helped to bind publicans and sinners in their sins.

But Jesus despaired of none of them. He hoped for all of them. And because of His hopefulness, He was able to redeem them. That hope of His kindled hope in them. They were lifted out of their lethargy and despair by the hope of Jesus. They were made to feel that it was possible even for them to rise to holiness and saintliness by the hope of Jesus. They were saved "by hope."

"Thou also art a son of Abraham," He said to Zacchæus; and the little man, who had hitherto thought himself doomed to the life of the swindler and the thief, when he heard that, publican though he was, it was possible for him to live the great and noble life that would put him in the succession to the father of the faithful, braced himself up on the spot and resolved by grace he would show himself worthy of that great faith of Christ. He was lifted out of the mire of sin and the slough of despond in which he had lain for so long by Christ's belief in him. He was "saved by hope."

This optimism of Jesus was an element in His redeeming power. And there was no limit to His redeeming power, because there was none beyond the limits of His hope. He was able to save to the uttermost, because He hoped to the uttermost.

Christ's Hope for Peter

Now it is just another illustration of the redeeming power of Christ's optimism that I find in this account of the call of Simon. First of all, notice that Christ knew Simon through and through. The word which our revisers translate "looked upon" denotes, as Godet says, "that penetrating glance which reaches to the very source of the individuality." It is the same word that is used to describe the look the maid gave Peter in the judgment hall. She gazed at him, she looked him up and down and then said, "Thou also wast with the Nazarene."

That was the kind of look Jesus gave Simon now; it was no mere casual glance; it was a searching scrutiny; Jesus "looked *into* Simon," so the phrase might be literally rendered; it was a gaze that pierced to the very roots of his character, that scanned his soul to its depths. And what did Christ see? A rash, hot, impulsive, unstable nature. He knew exactly the kind of man he was. He knew exactly the kind of reputation he had on the lake. He knew what men used to say of him—"that there was no depending on Simon, that it was just as well to have no dealings with him in the way of trade." He knew that by this deplorable weakness of his he had brought himself and his partners into trouble many a time. Jesus looked *into* Simon and read all that as plainly as we read a printed page. And in His first word He let Simon know He knew everything.

As Godet says again, it is the "look" that explains the following apostrophe. He "looked into" him and then said to him, "Thou art Simon, the son of John," as if to say, "I know quite well the character associated with that name. I know all that people say about you. I know your reputation on the lake. I know all about that weakness of yours that has so often put you to shame and made you bite the dust. I know all. Thou art Simon, the son of John."

But now, notice how Christ's glorious and superb optimism reveals itself. Knowing Simon as He does through and through, He dares to hope for him. Knowing all about his weakness, He yet has a super faith in him. "Thou art Simon, the son of John: thou shalt be called Cephas (which is by interpretation Peter)."

What magnificent optimism is this! Christ dares to hope that He can make a rock out of this man whose instability had passed into a proverb, whose weakness was his reproach and shame. And that splendid hope of Jesus helped to redeem and save Simon!

Yes, Simon was saved "by hope," his Lord's radiant and invincible hope in him and for him. For when Andrew brought him to Jesus that day, Simon was in the Slough of Despond. When his brother said to him, "We have found the Messiah," and brought him to Jesus, Simon in his heart did not think the message concerned him much. Of what use would he be to the Messiah? If He desired disciples, it was steady, reliable men like Andrew that He wanted, not weak, fickle, and unstable men like Simon who would perhaps break down at the first occasion of stress and trial. But our Lord's first word to him put new courage into his heart, new resolution into his soul, for it was a word of glorious and splendid hope. "Thou art Simon . . . thou shalt be . . . Peter!"

Now notice, Christ's optimism would not have helped Simon very much had it not been that he felt *it was the optimism of One who knew all*. Had it been nothing beyond the good-natured remark of a casual stranger, it would have brought no strength to Simon's soul. He would have said sorrowfully to himself, "He does not know my weakness and shame." But Simon felt Jesus had searched

him through and through. He felt those clear and steadfast eyes had looked into his inmost soul—that all things
lay naked and open before Him with whom he had to do.
And it was the certainty that Jesus knew all that lent
such redeeming energy to his hope. "Thou art Simon . . .
thou shalt be Peter," said Jesus, and at that Simon lifted
up his head and his heart. His redemption began at that
moment. Courage and high resolve entered into his heart
there and then. He was saved "by hope."

"Thou art . . . thou shalt be," in that contrast you have
the optimism, the redeeming optimism of Jesus. No man
can be a redeemer who has not a "shalt be" for the persons he seeks to redeem. Plato could not be a redeemer to
the poor and low-born of Greece; he had no "shalt be" for
them. Priests and scribes could not be redeemers to the
publicans and sinners of Palestine. They had no "shalt
be" for them.

There are plenty of people who can diagnose the condition of mankind today with exactness, who can point out
the ill and describe the malady, but they can do nothing to
redeem people because they know no cure. Thomas Hardy
can describe with terrible fidelity man's misery and woe,
but he can do little to redeem him; he has no "shalt be."

But Jesus Christ is fitted to be the world's Redeemer
just because He has a "shalt be" for every one. Taking us
just as we are, He tells us of something better and nobler
which by the grace of God we may become. "Thou art . . .
thou shalt be." He has a "shalt be" for us, no matter how
desperate and hopeless our case may appear to be. Knowing our weakness and shame, He speaks to us of a "shalt
be" of strength and honor and victory.

Think of the "shalt be's" He uttered to others. He found
Mary in her shame and spoke to her a "shalt be" of holiness and purity. He found Levi at his tollbooth and spoke
to him a "shalt be" of service and saintliness. He found
Saul, a blasphemer and persecutor and injurious, and
spoke to him a "shalt be" of grace and apostleship.

And the Christ who hoped for the harlot and the publican and the persecutor of long ago hopes still with an
invincible hope for the most abject and desperate of men.

He goes about this sad and stricken world whispering to the men and women who have lost heart and are down His "shalt be" that speaks of the dawn and the better day. "Thou art weak," He says to this one; "thou shalt be strong." "Thou art bound in affliction and iron," He says to another; "thou shalt be set at liberty." "Thou art vile and full of sin," he says to a third; "thou shalt be clean as a little child." "Thou art a prodigal among the swine . . . thou shalt be a son at home." And this "shalt be" of Christ's, this radiant optimism of His, lifts men out of their sloth and their sin and their despair. It makes "new men" of them. They are saved "by hope."

There are just two further words I wish to say about this redeeming optimism of Jesus.

The "Shalt Be" of Strength

First, notice how our Lord's "shalt be" met Simon's special need. Simon's shame was his weakness. The gift that Simon longed for, but despaired of getting, was *strength*. That is just the gift Jesus dares to hope for him. "Thou art Simon—weak, vacillating, irresolute . . . thou shalt be Peter . . . the rock." Jesus dares to hope and to prophesy for this man victory over his besetting sin. He dares to predict that just where he is weak there he shall become strong.

He speaks the same glorious "shalt be" to men still, because He cherishes the same radiant and unconquerable hope. Have you never met with those who have despaired of themselves because of the grip some passion has upon their souls? A young fellow came to me one day and told me of his craving for drink. He was only twenty-six years of age, and he said to me: "It's no use fighting against it; it's too strong for me." But Jesus never admits that any sin is too strong. He believes that every passion can be conquered, that every chain of habit can be broken. "Thou art a drunkard," He says; "thou shalt be sober." "Thou art a profligate; thou shalt be chaste." "Thou art a man of unclean lips; thou shalt be pure in heart." His "shalt be" is a message of hope addressed to our sorest need.

The "Shalt Be" Justified

And the second word I want to say is this—that Christ's optimism is an optimism abundantly justified. His "shalt be" is a "shalt be" that comes true. His "hope" is a hope that maketh not ashamed. "Thou shalt be . . . Peter," said Jesus; and I can imagine those who stood by and knew Simon's reputation turning away with a smile and perhaps a shrug of the shoulders. But it came true.

Look at this Simon in later days. Look at him before the Sanhedrin boldly preaching Christ to the men who had murdered Him. Look at him—according to the old legend—marching bravely back to Rome to lay down his life in his Master's cause. What do you see there? Simon become Peter . . . the rock. Christ's most daring "shalt be's" come true. His hope is no vain and treacherous hope. Here is an army of men and women whom He found plunged in sin and shame, beginning with the publicans and sinners in Palestine long ago and stretching down to those drinking and swearing colliers in South Wales whom by the thousand He has turned into sober and praying men—ready to attest that Christ's "shalt be's" all come true. Christ is the optimistic Christ to this day.

He is full of unquenchable hope for us. He knows all about our present state, and yet He speaks of a glorious and blessed future as being possible for us. "Thou art—" He says to each one of us; we can fill in the necessary description ourselves. But He adds, "Thou shalt be—." What? Well, tongue fails to tell what we shall be, but we know that when He shall be manifested, we shall be like Him, for we shall see Him as He is.

Don't Ever Lose Hope: You Can Be Changed

Aiden Wilson Tozer (1897–1963) was a self-taught preacher and theologian whose sermons and writings have greatly influenced the church around the world with their emphasis on personal holiness and the importance of glorifying God. He pastored Christian and Missionary Alliance churches in West Virginia, Ohio, Pennsylvania, and Indiana before becoming pastor of the Southside Alliance Church in Chicago in 1928. When a heart attack called him Home May 12, 1963, he was pastoring the Avenue Road Church in Toronto. For many years he edited *The Alliance Weekly,* later called *The Alliance Witness,* and his editorials have been compiled into many books.

This sermon is taken from *The Tozer Pulpit,* volume 7, edited by Gerald B. Smith and published by Christian Publications.

Aiden Wilson Tozer

3

DON'T EVER LOSE HOPE: YOU CAN BE CHANGED

> As obedient children, not fashioning yourselves according to the former lusts in your ignorance: but as he which hath called you is holy, so be ye holy in all manner of conversation (1 Peter 1:14–15).

THE CHRISTIAN CHURCH cannot effectively be Christ's church if it fails to firmly believe and boldly proclaim to every person in the human race: "You can be changed! You do not have to remain as you are!"

Brethren, this is not just a hope held out to the desperate dope addict and the helpless drunkard—it is the hope of every average sinner no matter where he may be found in the world.

Shall we heed what the Holy Spirit is trying to say to us about human nature and God's grace in this apostolic injunction?

"Not fashioning yourselves according to the former lusts"—here is a truth negatively stated but carrying with it a positive assertion. We all know from our studies how every concept carries its opposite along with it in its understanding.

For instance, if you say "short," the opposite, "long," is conjured up in the back of your mind. Otherwise, there would be no reason to call something short.

A Positive Pattern

Notice that the Apostle did not say, "Do not fashion yourselves . . ."—that would be contrary to Scripture and contrary to human nature.

His injunction is: Fashion not yourself after the old pattern, the pattern of your former lusts in your ignorance.

So, it is the positive element that we consider. Certainly and positively you will fashion yourselves, but do not fashion yourselves after the old pattern, we are cautioned.

This is at the insistence of the Holy Spirit, and the Scriptures give no room for argument here. We are given no excuse whatsoever to read this or sit in a church service and find fault with what the Holy Spirit says. You may have reason to disagree with an interpretation given by the preacher, but that is another matter. Once we know what the Holy Spirit has said, as believers we are committed to carry out that injunction without one word of objection. What else should we do with the Word of God but obey?

So, our English word, *fashion*, expresses the Apostle's admonition that Christian believers ought to shape themselves according to proper pattern.

"Fashion yourselves—conform yourselves to the right pattern" is what Peter was actually saying.

In essence, Peter was also stressing a most important fact, that human nature is fluid. Human nature is not fixed and unchangeable as many people seem to believe.

Perhaps clay is the very best illustration to give us a simple understanding of this biblical principle.

Clay is not fixed. It is malleable. In a figurative sense it is "fluid" so it can be shaped.

After clay has been fashioned and shaped by the potter, after he has given it the form that he wants, he puts it into the oven. He bakes it and burns it and then, perhaps, he glazes it.

That clay is now permanently fixed. It is no longer fluid, no longer subject to any changes. The only way it can be changed now is by being destroyed. It can be crushed and ruined, but it can never be changed into something more beautiful and useful because it can never regain its fluid and malleable state.

I believe, then, that the very fact that the Holy Spirit would indicate through the Apostle, "Fashion and shape yourselves after the right pattern," makes it plain that the burning and baking and glazing have not yet happened to human nature. Thankfully we are in a state of fluidity regarding moral character.

The Hope of Change

Now, there are two things that can be said about any person, whether it is a youngster or the man sitting in the death cell of the state prison awaiting his fate for kidnapping and murder.

The first thing that can be said is: "You can be changed!" The second thing is like unto it: "You are not finished yet!"

We hear a lot about men being hardened, but we should always remember that we need modifiers if we are going to get at the truth.

When we say that a man is hardened and that he is beyond help, we are saying that insofar as any power and influence that we may have, the man is probably in a state beyond our changing.

But actually and in truth, no one is beyond changing as long as he is alive and conscious!

The hope may be dim in many cases, but the hope of change does exist for every man. It may be a dim hope for the drunkard who allows himself only a few sober moments for serious thought, but he may be saved from complete despair by the knowledge that he can be changed.

It is still a hope even for the drug addict who is in frightful misery and who would sell his own soul to get the shot or the fix to carry him through one more day. The only reason he does not commit suicide is that faint flicker of hope that he can still be changed. He knows that he has not yet been cast or glazed in a final, unchangeable state—there is still a fluidity.

Let us thank God that there is that kind of hope and the possibility of great change even for those who would likely be written off by our own human judgment. History has truly and completely confirmed this possibility.

The blessed aspect of this truth is that there is no sinner anywhere in the world who is compelled to remain as he is today.

He may be floundering in his sin, so deeply enmeshed

that he is ashamed of himself. But the very fact that he is ashamed indicates that there is a model and a pattern to which he may still attain. It is this hope of change that keeps men alive on the earth.

The second part of this ray of hope for any man is the prospect that he is not yet "finished."

I dare to say that whoever you are and wherever you may be, old or young or in between, you are not yet a finished product. You are only in process.

I admit that it is our human tendency to fix certain terminal points and to say, "Beyond these we do not go."

Take human birth for instance.

Looking at birth in one way, we recognize that the obstetrician, after examining the new baby and finding it healthy, may say: "Now this is fixed. As far as I am concerned, a child is born into the world, and my part is complete." He fixes a terminal point there and goes about his other concerns.

During the months just preceding, he was very anxious and concerned. For him, the terminal point has now been reached—a healthy, normal child has been born into the world.

But the mother of the child does not join in any terminal point at this juncture. She knows there is a tiny life involved, and she knows the long continuing process which lies ahead. She knows of the childhood problems and troubles. She knows the educational process ahead from the time she teaches him to play patty-cake until he walks out of the college hall with his degree. The child is not "fixed"—there is the long process of shaping and fashioning.

Then when he has gotten his college degree, the parents are likely to rejoice and fix their own terminal point: "Well, we have succeeded in getting him through college!" Parents have a tendency to put a period there and say, "Now he is finished. He is complete."

But beyond all of that we know the truth—he is not done. He is not finished. There are still many changes to come, and he is still being shaped and fashioned.

There will soon be another terminal point—his marriage. Many a mother breathes a sigh of relief when the child suddenly becomes serious, settles down, gets married, establishes a home.

Her sigh is really her way of saying within: "Now my worries are over!"

But not everything and everyone that is settled down is finished either. Parents are gratified when success comes and their boy becomes vice president of his company, drawing a big check and driving an expensive car.

The parents smile at each other and say, "Now he is fixed. He has arrived. He is a big American businessman!" It is not easy for parents to look beyond this pleasant terminal point.

But their child is still moving along. He will come to middle age when, as the poet said, "Gray hairs are here and there upon him." The parents comment that his gray hairs really give him a distinguished look, and they cannot conceive that things will ever really change for him.

"He has really arrived," is their consolation. "He is a portly, well-proportioned businessman, an executive. He hunts in the fall and fishes in the spring and goes to baseball games in the summer—all the things that professional businessmen do. Don't worry about him. He is fixed!"

But he is a human being, and he is not fixed. He will never be finished until the soul leaves the body. Even the old man in his dotage is still changing in some ways. The rapidity and scope of change may not be as great, but there is change nevertheless.

A Continued Process

It is at this point that someone will want to establish a dialogue. Someone will say, "Oh, yes, Mr. Tozer, but I do know a terminal point. You have been talking in terms of humanity, unregenerate humanity. The fixed point, the terminal point is the time of our conversion to Christ."

Yes, there is a point there when we can say, "Now rest my long-divided heart, fixed on this blissful center, rest!"

But does our conversion to Christ and our assurance of forgiveness mean that the fluidity in our nature is gone and that we are finally "fixed"?

My friend, the answer is "No!" You are still fluid. You are still subject to being fashioned and changed and shaped. God expects that you will still grow and develop and change and be fashioned as a Christian in maturity and Christlikeness.

Peter was recognizing that Christian believers are still in process when he wrote, "Do not fashion yourselves after the old pattern but after a new and holy pattern!"

I think there are many followers of Christ who have never been brought into this realization and understanding. Perhaps Christian workers are at fault at this point, when we work so hard to get people converted and then put a period after their conversion and speak the comfortable words: "Now rest your long-divided heart!"

There is a sense in which that old hymn is beautifully, brilliantly true, and I love it and sing it often. But I am sure that the writer was not intending to imply a terminal point. I am sure he was not suggesting that the believer is no longer fluid, malleable. The fact is that he was assuring us that our being fixed in Christ is settled by an act of faith—and that's what we mean. But when it comes to the shaping and developing and growth and enlargement—these must go on after we are converted!

I expect some objections here from the people who would insist that Christians cannot fashion themselves.

"God must fashion us. God is our heavenly Father, and He must do the fashioning and changing," they point out.

Let me agree this far: that is the ideal and that is the way it *should* be.

If every believer could be completely and wholly surrendered from the moment he is saved until the time he dies, knowing nothing but the influences of God and the heavenly powers working in him, then that would be true.

But there are powers that shape men even in the kingdom of God, that are not divine powers.

Let me use an illustration here of the person interested in getting a suntan, exposing himself to the sun at the beach or in his own back yard.

Now, who is tanning his hide? Where is the tan coming from? What does the person himself have to do with it?

There is a sense in which he is doing it, for if he had kept his shirt on, his shoulders and body would never be tanned.

But there is a sense in which the sun is doing it. The sun is tanning him, but he had to take the necessary step to cooperate with the rays of the sun in order for the sunlight to do its work.

Now, that is exactly what we mean when we say that we fashion ourselves. A Christian believer fashions himself by exposing himself to the divine powers which shape him. Just as a man may wear his jacket and never get the suntan even though the sun is up there brightly in view, so a Christian may keep himself wrapped in a cloak of his own stubbornness and never receive any of the beneficial graces which filter down from the throne of God where Jesus sits as mediator.

Yes, it is possible for a Christian to go through life without very much change taking place. Converted? Yes. A believer in Christ? Yes. Having the root of the matter in him? Yes. The Deed of God in him? Yes.

But such a believer is infantile, and the growth and development and beautifying and enlarging and shaping have not taken place because he refuses to cooperate and expose himself to the divine powers that would shape him.

A Conflict of Powers

The reverse side of this proposition must also be considered. It is entirely possible for the Christian believer to shape himself by exposing himself to the wrong kind of influences. I think this is happening to an extent that must indeed be a grievance to God.

Now, what about these powers that can fashion us?

We know full well what the old powers were. Those old powers were the "former lusts."

The Apostle soberly reminds us of those powers in the second chapter of Ephesians:

"Wherein in time past ye walked according to the course of this world, according to the prince of the power of the air, the spirit that now worketh in the children of disobedience; among whom also we all had our conversation in times past in the lusts of our flesh, fulfilling the desires of the flesh and of the mind; and were by nature the children of wrath, even as others" (2:2-3).

Those were the forces which had a part in shaping us in our past. But now, even though weary, worn, and sad, we have come to the Savior and found in Him a resting place. And He has made us glad!

Therefore, we are encouraged to put away those old forces. We are not to expose ourselves to them any more.

But the question is often raised: "How can I hold myself from being shaped? I am thrown daily among the people of this world. I work in a situation where men are wicked and vulgar and obscene."

Here's my answer: You must engage your own will in the direction of God's will for your life. You can keep yourself from being shaped by your situation just as a man on the beach can keep himself from being tanned by the sun. You can draw your being tightly up in faith by an act of your will and take a positive stand: "Stay out, you devilish influences, in the name of my Savior! Let my soul alone—it belongs to God!"

Many of our students can tell of the dirty talk and irreverence in their schools. Some of our Christian young people have even found a way to turn those things to personal spiritual blessing. Hearing an obscenity, they have an instant reaction and a compensation within: "Oh, God, I hate that so much that I want You to make my own mind and speech cleaner than it ever was before!"

Seeing an injurious, wicked habit in others, they look within at once and breathe a silent prayer: "Oh, God, You are able to keep me and shield me from this thing!"

It is possible, even in this sensuous world with its emphasis on violence and filth, that we can use those very things and react or compensate in the direction of God's promised victory. We are assured in the Word of God that we do not have to yield in weakness to the pull that would drag us down.

When we see something that we know is wrong and displeasing to Him, we can react to it with a positive assurance as we say: "God helping me, I will be different from that!" In that sense, the very sight of evil can drive us farther into the kingdom of God.

A Pattern to Follow

Now, what can we put into practice from this approach?

I share with you a few very simple thoughts about basic things in our own day that have powers to shape us, whether or not we are Christians. These are everyday things, and they have influence upon our lives whether we know it or not, whether we believe it or not, or whether we like it or not.

What can you say about the kinds of books and magazines you read? The things you read will fashion you by slowly conditioning your mind. Little by little, even though you think you are resisting, you will take on the shape of the mind of the author of that book you are reading. You will begin to put your emphasis where he puts his. You will begin to put your values where he places his. You will find yourself liking what he likes and thinking as he thinks.

The same thing is certainly true of the power of modern films on the minds and morals of those who give themselves over to their influences.

Then, what about the kind of music you enjoy?

It seems almost too late in these times to try to give a warning that many in our society seem to revel in—the vile and vicious and obscene words of gutter songs. But there are other accepted types of music just as dangerous and just as damaging to the human spirit, just as harmful to the soul.

It is not overstating the case to insist that the kinds of music you enjoy will demonstrate pretty much what you are like inside.

If you give yourself to the contemporary fare of music that touches the baser emotions, it will shape your mind and emotions and desires whether you admit it or not.

You can drink poison if you want to, but I am still friend enough to warn you that if you do, you will be carried out in a box. I cannot stop you but I can warn you. Nor do I have authority to tell you what you should listen to, but I have a divine commission to tell you that if you love and listen to the wrong kinds of music, your inner life will wither and die.

Think with me also about the kind of pleasures in which you indulge.

If we should start to catalog some of your pastimes, you would probably break in and ask: "What's wrong with this?" and "What's wrong with that?"

There probably is no answer that will completely satisfy you if you are asking the question, but this is the best answer: "Give a person ten years in the wrong kind of indulgence and questionable atmosphere and see what happens to the inward spiritual life."

The pleasures in which we indulge selfishly will shape us and fashion us over the years, for whatever gives us pleasure has the subtle power to change us and enslave us.

What are the fond ambitions you entertain for your life?

The dream of whatever you would like to be will surely influence and shape you. It will also lead to choices of the places where you spend your time. I realize that we are not going to be very successful in advising people where they should go and should not go. Just the same, those who are on their way to heaven through faith in God's Son and God's plan should be careful of the kind of places they frequent, because these will shape and leave their imprint on man's spirit and soul.

We would do well to consider also the kind of words we speak.

Of all the people in the world I have read about, I think American people must be the most careless with language and expression.

For instance, any typical American joke must be an exaggeration. Mark Twain used the device of exaggeration, and it has become an accepted form not only of comedy but of communication among Americans. Are you watching your own language and are you careful of your own expressions in view of what it could mean to the effectiveness of your own Christian testimony?

Next, consider how important it is to make and cherish the right kind of friends in this life.

I value friendship very highly. I know we can appreciate and honor one another in friendship even in this wicked world.

Because it is possible that friendships can be beautiful and helpful, I have always felt something like a churlish heel to stand before an audience and insist: "You must break off certain friendships if you want to truly serve God."

But our Lord Jesus said it more plainly and more bluntly than I could ever say it. He told us that in being His disciples we must take up our cross and follow Him, and there would be instances when we must turn our backs on those who would hold us back—even our own relatives and close friends. Jesus Christ must be first in our hearts and minds, and it is He who reminds us that the salvation of our souls is of prime importance.

Better to have no friends and be an Elijah, alone, than to be like Lot in Sodom, surrounded by friends who all but damned him. If you give your cherished friendship to the ungodly counselor and the scorner, you have given the enemy the key to your heart. You have opened the gate, and the city of your soul will be overwhelmed and taken!

Finally, what kind of thoughts do we spend our time brooding over?

It is quite evident that for every murder or robbery, an embezzlement or other evil deeds, someone has spent long hours brooding over the idea, the plans, the chance of gain, or the hope of revenge. In our great increasing wave of crime and violence, every deed is conditioned or preceded by some brooding thoughts.

Whatever thoughts you are willing to breed over in the night seasons will shape you and form you. The thoughts you entertain can change you from what you are into something else, and it will not be for the better unless your thoughts are good thoughts.

In the light of all these influences, Paul appeals to us all: "Be not conformed . . . but be transformed!" You do have a soul and you have influences that will shape you. God gives the clay to the potter and says, "Now, shape it!"

God gives the material to the builder and says, "Now, build it into a worthy temple!"

Then, God says at last, "How did you shape it? How did you fashion it? What do you have to bring me from the material that I gave you? What did you do with those forces and influences that came to you daily?"

I trust that in that last great day none of us will have to stand before the judgment seat of Christ and confess with shame that we allowed unworthy things to have a place in shaping our lives.

Rather, it is time now to be transformed by the renewing of our minds that we may know what is the perfect and acceptable will of God!

NOTES

The Heroism of Endurance

Hugh Black (1868–1953) was born and trained in Scotland and ministered with Alexander Whyte at Free St. George's in Edinburgh. He served as professor of Homiletics at Union Theological Seminary, New York (1906–1938), and was widely recognized as a capable preacher.

This sermon is taken from *Listening to God* by Hugh Black, published in 1906 by Fleming H. Revell Company, New York.

Hugh Black

4

THE HEROISM OF ENDURANCE

If thou hast run with the footmen, and they have wearied
thee, then how canst thou contend with horses? and though
in a land of peace thou art secure, yet how wilt thou do in
the pride of Jordan? (Jeremiah 12:5, RV).

WE GET MANY glimpses into the personality of Jeremiah.
Though the story of his life is fragmentary, we can read
the story of his heart. Again and again we see something
which reveals his inner nature. We see a timid, shrinking
man in process of hardening to be made the prophet required for his generation. That character, keen and strong
like well-tempered steel, was formed in the fire. It was
ever through the furnace of living pain. Of all the martyr-
doms of the Bible—and it is a long record of martyr-
doms—there is none so unrelieved as this one.

Christ had keener sorrow, but He also had keener joy.
He had a hope which was assurance. He knew that His
blood would be the seed of the church. Whatever the
present might have been to Him, He had always the future. "For the joy that was set before Him He endured the
cross, despising the shame."

Jeremiah escaped pangs that only the pure heart of
Christ could feel, but he was forced by the facts of his age
to utter a message that had few notes of hope. He lived on
till he was an old man and saw the calamities he had
himself predicted. His eyes, that had wept over the Holy
City, saw it sacked and depopulated. He had to witness
the fulfillment of his own words of doom. Unless we can
enter with some sympathy into the sort of man Jeremiah
was by nature, unless we can understand the man, we
cannot understand the book. Once and again he wished to
give up the task as too heavy a burden for him to bear;
but ever he was braced to face his destiny once more with
clear eye and stern brow.

Lonely at the Top

In the present instance we see the prophet's education going on. We see him being hardened in the fire like a Damascus blade. In a mood of depression, sick with his failure in the great city, he longs for the quiet village hallowed by the peaceful days of his youth. He turns to home like a tired bird to its nest, as a wounded beast drags himself to his lair—to find in the nest a scorpion! His fellow-townsmen, even his brethren and the house of his father, even they dealt treacherously with him. He is learning the *loneliness of life at the high altitudes.* The ordinary forms of good and evil easily find comradeship. Men shudder at an exceptional evil and shrink from an exceptional good. Not everyone wants to breathe the foul vapors of the pit; not everyone can breathe the rarefied air of the heights. Commonplace good and evil attract crowds according to their kind. Jeremiah had to pay the price of singularity. He had to learn not only to do without the sweet incense of popular favor but also to stand unflinching even when it turned into the hot breath of hatred. He had to submit not only to be without friends but to see friends become foes.

This experience through which the prophet passed is a cruel one. It either makes a man, or mars him, and nearly always hardens him. It creates an indignation, a holy anger sometimes against men, sometimes against the strange untoward state of affairs, sometimes against God. It has made some raise blasphemous voice and impious hand. Such an experience is always presented with the temptation, which came to Job, to curse God and die. The injustice of it rankles in the heart, unless the heart is bent humbly and inquiringly to God to learn what the true meaning of the visitation may be.

Jeremiah here is kicking against the pricks which have wounded the feet of men for centuries, how to account for the fact that in a world governed by a righteous God, righteousness should often have to suffer so much. But in the midst of the cruel experience he never lets go his grip of God. "Righteous art Thou, O God," he says—whatever comes, that is the first established fact of life. "Yet," he continues in holy boldness, "let me reason with Thee of Thy judgments. Wherefore doth the wicked prosper? Wherefore are all they at peace that deal treacherously?" His indignant soul, on fire for justice, cries out that it ought not to be so. But the undercurrent of the complaint is not the seeming prosperity of the wicked but his own pain and sorrow and terrible adversity.

We do not ask a solution of the universe, till we are forced to ask a solution of our own place and lot in it. God's providence seemed perfect to Job, till he was caught in the tempest and tossed aside broken. We are not much concerned about mere abstract injustice. Jeremiah's *wherefore* about the wicked is really a *why* about himself. Why am I bared to the blast in following Thy will and performing Thy command? Why are tears and strife my portion? Why am I wearied out and left desolate, though I am fighting the Lord's battle? That is the prophet's real complaint.

The Heroism of Endurance

Notice the answer, surely the strangest and most inconsequent ever given. There is no attempt at explanation. God never explains Himself in a ready-made fashion. God explains Himself through life. God explains Himself by deeds. The complaint here is answered by a countercomplaint. Jeremiah's charge against God of injustice is met by God's charge against Jeremiah of weakness. "If thou hast run with the footmen, and they have wearied thee, then how canst thou contend with horses? If in the land of peace thou art secure, how wilt thou do (O fainthearted one!) in the pride of Jordan?" The "Pride of Jordan" means the dangerous ground by the river, where the heat is almost tropical and the vegetation is rank. It is jungle, tangled bush where wild beasts lurk, leopards and wolves and (at that time also) lions.

The answer to the complaint against the hardness of his lot is simply the assertion that it shall be harder still. He has only been running with footmen so far—he will have to contend with horses, when he may have cause to speak of weariness. He has only been living in a land of peace so far—he will have to dwell in the jungle where are wild beasts, and then he may talk of danger.

Does it seem an unfeeling answer? It was the answer Jeremiah needed. He needed to be braced, not pampered. He is taught the need of endurance. It is a strange cure for cowardice, a strange remedy for weakness; yet it is effective. It gives stiffening to the soul. The tear-stained face is lifted up calm once more. A new resolution creeps into the eye to prove worthy of the new responsibility. God appeals to the strength in Jeremiah, not to the weakness. By God's grace I will fight, and fighting fall if need be. By God's grace I will contend even with horses; I will go to the pride of Jordan though the jungle growl and snarl. This was the result on Jeremiah, and it was the result required. Only a heroic soul could do the heroic work needed by Israel and by God, and it was the greatest heroism of all which was needed, the *heroism of endurance*.

Nothing worth doing can be done in this world without something of that iron resolution. It is the spirit which never knows defeat, which cannot be worn out, which has taken its stand and refuses to move. This is the "patience" about which the Bible is full, not the sickly counterfeit which so often passes for patience, but the power to bear, to suffer, to sacrifice, to endure all things, to die, harder still sometimes to continue to live. The whole world teaches that patience. Life in her struggle with nature is lavish of her resources. She is willing to sacrifice anything for the bare maintenance of existence meanwhile. Inch by inch each advance has to be gained, fought for, paid for, kept. It is the lesson of all history also, both for the individual and for a body of men who have espoused any cause.

Christ's church has survived through her power to endure. She was willing to give up anything to hold her ground, willing to pour out blood like water in order to take root. The mustard seed, planted with tears and watered with blood, stood the hazard of every storm, gripped tenaciously the soil, twining its roots round the rocks, reared its head ever a little higher, and spread out its branches ever a little fuller, and when the tempest came held on for very life; then, never hasting, never resting, went on in the divine task of growing; at last became the greatest of trees, giving shelter to the birds of the air in its wide-spreading branches.

So is the kingdom of heaven. It is a true parable of the church. She conquered violence, not by violence but by virtue. She overcame force, not by force but by patience. Her sons were ready to die—to die daily—to run with footmen and then to contend with horses. It was given unto them not only to believe in Christ but to suffer for His sake. They could not be stamped out. When their persecutors thought they were scattered like chaff, it turned out that they were scattered like seed. The omnipotent power of Rome was impotent before such resolution. The battle is the place to make soldiers, not the barracks. The church met the empire and broke it through the sheer power to endure. She was willing to suffer and to suffer and to suffer—and afterward to conquer.

It is the same secret of success for the individual spiritual life. "In your patience ye shall win your souls." This method is utterly opposed to the world's method of insuring success which is by self-assertion, aggressive action, force for force, blow for blow. Patience, not violence, is the Christian's safety. Even if all else be lost, it saves the soul, the true life. It gives fiber to the character. It purifies the heart as gold in the furnace. "Violence does even justice unjustly," says Carlyle—which was a great admission for him who worshiped might of any kind even when displayed in violence. The church wearied out the empire and then absorbed it. And it was only when she forgot her Master's method and adopted the world's method, wielding the secular sword, that she grew weak. This is Christ's plan of campaign for the church and for the individual. "He that endureth to the end shall be saved."

What do we know of this heroic endurance? In our fight with temptation, in our warfare against all forms of evil, have we used our Master's watchword and practiced our Master's scheme? Think of our temptation in the matter of Foreign Missions, for example. It is often looked on as a burden, something we must do because it has come to be expected as a sort of duty. It is not a fire in our bones which will give us no peace. It is not a task to which we feel we have been sent. We do not realize that Christ's soul is straitened till it be accomplished. We are easily made faint-hearted about it. We say that results are disproportionate to the effort; or rather (for that is not true) we are overpowered by the vastness of the work. If we find our small attempt a burden, how can we face the vaster problem of making the kingdoms of this world the kingdom of God and His Christ? If we are wearied in our race with footmen, how can we contend with horses?

We are so easily dispirited, not only in Christian enterprise but also in personal Christian endeavor. We are so soon tempted to give up. The enemy is too hard to dislodge; a besetting sin in our lives is too stubborn; a rampant evil in our community is too deeply rooted; the beautiful kingdom of heaven of our dreams is an impossible task. Fainthearted cravens that we are, what are we here in this world for? To find a land of peace in which to be secure? To look for a soft place? To find an easy task? To match ourselves against some halting footmen?

We need some iron in our blood. We need to be braced to the conflict again. We need the noble scorn of consequence. What have we done, the best of us, for God or for man? What have we endured for the dream's sake? What have we given up in our self-indulgent life? What sacrifice have we ever made? The folly of holding out for a little and at last giving up and letting the truth slip from our fingers! The folly of beginning in the spirit and at last ending miserably in the flesh! "Ye have not resisted unto blood, fighting against sin."

Is there to be no end to the warfare and the weariness? Is there to be no end in the individual struggle and in the social endeavor? Must Jeremiah harden himself forever and stiffen himself ever to endure? Must we resist forever the sins of our own hearts? Must we protest forever against the evil of the world? *Forever*, if need be! To begin to serve God is to serve Him forever. It knows no cessation. Complainings die in His presence, and we are sent out again, Christ's belted knights—His forever.

If God send a man to contend with horses, it is well. If God send a man to the pride of Jordan, it is well. He will not go alone. A land of peace without God is a terror. The jungle of Jordan with God is peace. Never a soul is tempted above what it can bear. Never a life is defeated that arms itself with the whole armor of God.

Lift up the hands which hang down and strengthen the feeble knees and make straight paths for your feet. "My grace is sufficient for you."

Blessed Hope

Dwight Lyman Moody (1837–1899) is known around the world as one of America's most effective evangelists. Converted as a teenager through the witness of his Sunday school teacher, Moody became active in YMCA and Sunday school work in Chicago while pursuing a successful business career. He then devoted his full time to evangelism and was used mightily of God in campaigns in both the United States and Great Britain. He founded the Northfield School for girls, the Mount Hermon School for boys, the Northfield Bible Conference, and the Moody Bible Institute in Chicago. Before the days of planes and radio, Moody traveled more than a million miles and addressed more than 100 million people.

This message is from *The Best of Dwight L. Moody*, edited by Ralph Turnbull and published in 1971 by Baker Book House.

Dwight Lyman Moody

5

BLESSED HOPE

But sanctify the Lord God in your hearts: and be ready always to give an answer to every man that asketh you a reason of the hope that is in you with meekness and fear (1 Peter 3:15).

I HAVE SELECTED for my subject this afternoon the blessed hope. We are told to be ready to give a reason for the hope we have within us, and what we want to do is to find out what our hope is. I believe there are a great many people who are hoping and hoping when they have no ground for hope. I don't know of any better way to find out whether we have true ground for the hope we have within us than to look in Scripture to see what the Scripture has to say.

Now, faith is one thing, and hope is another. "When hope takes the place of faith, it is a snare." Faith is to work and trust. Someone has said that life is to enjoy and obey and be like God; but hope is to wait and trust, to wait and expect—in other words, that hope is the daughter of faith. I heard a very godly man once say that joy was like the larks that sang in the morning when it was light, but hope was like the nightingale that sang in the dark; so that hope was really better than joy.

Most anyone can sing in the morning when everything is bright and everything going well; but hope sings in the dark, in the mist and the fog; it looks through all the mist and darkness into the clear day. Faith lays hold of what is in the Scripture; faith is laying hold of that which is within the veil and what is in heaven for us.

Now, we cannot get on any better without hope than we can without faith. The farmer who sows his seed sows it in the hope of a harvest; the merchant buys his goods in the hope to find customers, and the student toils in the hope that he will reap by-and-by.

Now, I want to call your attention to the three classes of people who are gathered here today. They are those who have no hope, those who have a false hope, and those who have a good hope. I do not know that there is anyone here today who would come under the first head. It is pretty hard to find anyone in this world who does not have some hope. Once in a while you will come across a person who has no hope in this life or the life to come. It is from that class that our suicides come. When men or women get to that point that they have no hope in this life, they become utterly discouraged, cast down, no hope in the life to come. They believe when they die that is the last of them. They are atheists in their views, believe there is no hereafter, put an end to their existence.

Those with No Hope

The point I want to call your attention to in the class that has no earthly hope is this, "A child is sick; a doctor is called, and he looks at the child and says there is no hope; but the moment the mother loses hope of the child living in this world, another hope comes up; she hopes to see the child again in another world. Hope comes and cheers that mother in trouble."

When Mr. Curtin was governor of Pennsylvania, a young man in that state was convicted of murder and was sentenced to be hung. His friends tried in every way they could to get him released. The young man was holding on to a hope that he would be released; they could not make him believe that he had to die. At last the governor sent for George H. Stuart and said to him, "I wish you would go down to that jail and tell that young man there is no hope; tell him that there is not one ray of hope, that on the day appointed he must die, that I am not going to pardon him." Mr. Stuart said when he went into the jail the young man's countenance lit up and he said, "Ah, I am sure you brought me good news. What does it say?"

Mr. Stuart said he would never be the bearer of such a message again. He said that he sat down beside him on the iron bed and said, "My friend, I am sorry to tell you there is not any hope. The governor says you must die at the appointed time. He will not pardon you. He sent me down here to take away this false hope you have got and to tell you you have to die." He said the young man fainted away, and it was some time before they could bring him to. The poor man's heart was broken.

He had been holding on to a false hope. In that case, that young man was not without hope, because he could repent, for God does forgive murderers, and become a child of God—become a saved man. Hope comes right in there. Even these men who think that they have no hope, there is hope for them if they will only turn to the God of hope and to the God of the Bible.

That is only one class. Job speaks about days passing without hope; but then he does not mean that there was not any hope beyond this life, because Job says in another place, "I know my Redeemer liveth, and that I shall see Him." He was like Paul. He knew in whom he believed. He had a hope in the darkness and fog; when those waves of persecution came dashing up against him and in the midst of the storm and conflict you could hear Job cry out, "I know my Redeemer liveth." He had a hope. So I say it is hard to find anyone that comes under the first head. Most people have some sort of hope.

Those with False Hope

Now I come to the second head, people who have a false hope. I contend that a man or woman who is resting in false hope is really worse off than one who has no hope in this world, because if a man wakes up to the fact that he has no hope, there is a chance of rousing him to seek a hope that is worth having. The moment you begin to talk with these men who have a false hope, they run right off into their fortress and say, "I am all right; I have got a hope." You can hardly find a man or woman in all this city today who has not a hope. But how many are resting in a false hope—a miserable, treacherous hope that is good for nothing? You can't find a drunkard who has not a hope. He hangs on to the rumbottle with one hand and hope with the other; his hope is a miserable lie; it is a refuge of lies that he has hid behind. You can't find a harlot who walks the streets of this city but that has some hope. You can hardly find a thief but who has some hope.

Now, what we want to do is to examine ourselves and see whether we have a hope that will stand the test of the judgment. We want to know whether we have a true hope or a false hope. If it is a false hope, the quicker we find it out the better. We don't want to be resting in a false hope. That has caused nearly all the mischief we have had in this country during the past few years. All these default-ers have come from that class. They were trusting in a false hope. They said, "I will take a little from the bank or from my employer. I will just overdraw my account a few thousand dollars, but I will replace it." But they went on drawing out and drawing out, and this false hope kept saying, "I can make it all right in a few days." They were led on and on by false hope until at last they got beyond hope and could not pay it back. They were ruined. They were not only ruined—it would be a good thing if they stopped there, but look at their wives and their children and their relatives, their parents and their loved ones that they have ruined. They didn't intend to become ru-ined men. They didn't intend to bring a blight upon their families and upon their prospects here. A false hope led them on step by step.

Now, my friends, let us be honest with ourselves today and ask ourselves honestly before God and man, "What is my hope?" Well, there is a lady up there in the gallery who says, "I joined the Methodist church ten years ago." Very well, suppose you did, what is your hope today? "Well, my hope is all right; I joined the church." But that is not going to stand the light of eternity. It doesn't say that you have to join some church. A man or woman may belong to a church and have not the spirit of Jesus Christ.

Yes, and another one says over there, "I have a better hope than that; I belong to the Congregational church and go out to all the meetings." A person may go to all the meetings and not have a true hope. Do you know that? If you allow the meetings to take the place of Jesus Christ and let the church come in, the denomination that you belong to, and take the place of Jesus Christ, you are resting on a rotten foundation and are building your house on a sandy foundation. When the storms come, the house will fall.

Nothing but Jesus Christ will do. But these false hopes will be swept away by-and-by. God's hail will sweep away the refuges of lies. It says in the eleventh chapter of Proverbs and seventh verse, "The hope of the unrighteous man perisheth." Now, if I belong to the church and am unrighteous, I may have a hope, but that is going to perish; and it may be I will not find it out until it is too late to get a good hope. It is a good deal better to find it out here today, when I have a chance to repent of my sin and turn to God and get a true hope, than it is to go with my eyes closed in the delusion that I am coming out all right.

There is another passage here in Job, twenty-seventh chapter and eighth verse, "For what is the hope of the hypocrite, though he hath gained, when God taketh away his soul?" What is his hope good for? The hope of the hypocrite is not good for anything. A man may gain by his hypocrisy; a man may put on the garb of religion and profess to be what he is not and may gain by it; there is no doubt of that; some do that, and they gain a little. But what shall it profit a man if he does gain by his hypocrisy, and God takes away his soul? His hope is gone. It was a treacherous hope. It was good for nothing.

"But then," you may say, "I am not an unrighteous man; I don't come under that head at all, and I am no hypocrite." Well, I am afraid a good many of us who think we are not hypocrites are more or less hypocrites after all. The trouble is, men are trying to pass themselves off for more than they are worth. They are trying to make people believe they are better than they really are. God wants honesty. God wants downright uprightness, if you will allow me the expression. He wants us to be truthful and upright in all our transactions. If we are not, our profession doesn't help us. You may belong to this church or to that church. You may. say your prayers, and you may go through the form of religion, but it will not help you.

What is the hope of the hypocrite when God shall take

away his soul? Suppose he has gained by his hypocrisy, there is not a thing, I believe, that God detests more than He does hypocrisy. He detests that sin more than He does all others. Jesus tore away the false hope of some of His disciples and told them, "Except your righteousness exceed the righteousness of the Scribes and Pharisees, ye shall in no wise enter into the kingdom of God." Ah, there will be many a man and many a woman, I am afraid, by-and-by, who will wake up and find their hope has been a false one after all.

Then there is another hope that is false. Men say, "I think God is very merciful, and that it will come out all right in the end." God has declared with an oath that He will not clear the guilty. What folly it is for a man to stand up and say, "I know I swear now and then; but then God don't mean anything when He says I shan't swear. God is only winking at sin. It will come out all right. The blasphemer, the drunkard, the libertine, and the man who is vile and polluted in heart will be just the same at the end of the route. That is my hope." Well, it is a false hope. If there is a drunkard here today, let me tell you that your hope is perfectly worthless, because God says that no drunkard shall inherit the kingdom of heaven. That we find not only in the Old Testament but in the New.

And if there is a man here who sells liquor—that is party to the hellish act of putting the bottle in his neighbor's hand, there is not any hope for him. I don't care how much money you give to help build your churches. I don't care if you have the best pew in one of your large churches and walk down the broad aisle every Sunday with your wife and children and take your seat there. "Woe be to the man that putteth the bottle to his neighbor's lips." God has pronounced a curse against that man. Things look altogether different when we stand before the judge of all the earth.

Yes, but then there is another man. He says, "I can go on as I am, and by-and-by when I am sick, I can repent on my deathbed." I think that is a false hope. And let me say, I think there is any quantity of lying in the sickroom, a good many false hopes held out to the sick. Here is a person dying, and the doctor comes in. He knows very well that the disease is fatal and knows that person can't live ten days, and he says, "I think you will be well and out in a few days, in the course of thirty days." He knows very well it is death. They say to these consumptives when they see that awful look in the face; when they see his form is wasting, they say, "Well, think you will be out again in the spring; when the flowers begin to blossom, and nature begins to unfold itself, you will be out again," when they know it is downright lying.

O, the false hopes that are held out to sick and the dying! Then at the funeral people will stand up and pronounce a eulogy over a man who died in his sins when there is not a chance for his soul. God says, "The soul that sinneth it shall die." He has not sought eternal life. He has spurned the gift of God and trampled the Bible under his feet. Look at the lying at funerals, false hopes that are held out. What God wants is to have us real, as He is real, and if our hope is not a hope that will stand the test of eternity, then the quicker we find it out the better.

Then there is another false hope which I think is worse, perhaps, than any other, and that is that a man can repent beyond the grave. There is a class of people who say, "I can go on in my sins and live as I am living, and I can repent beyond the grave." Now, if there is a chance for a man to repent beyond the grave, I can't find it between the lids of the Bible. I believe that if a man dies in his sin, he is banished from God. And I believe that when Jesus Christ said, "If ye die in your sins, where I am ye cannot come," He meant what He said.

So, if our hope is false, let us find it out today. Let us be honest with ourselves and ask God to show it to us. If our hope is not on the solid rock, if we are building our house on the sand, let us find it out. You may say, "My hope is as good as yours. My house is as good-looking a house as yours." That may be. It might be a better looking house than mine. But the important thing is the foundation. What we want is to be sure that we have a good foundation.

A man may build up a very good character, but he may not have it on a good foundation. If he is building a house on the sand, when storm and trials come, down will come all his hopes. A false hope is worse than no hope. If you have a false hope today, make up your mind that you will not rest until you reach a hope that is worth having.

Now, here is a test that I think we can put to ourselves. If we have the Spirit of Jesus Christ, our life will be like His; that is, we will be humble, loving. We will not be jealous, will not be ambitious, self-seeking, covetous, revengeful. But we will be meek, tenderhearted, affectionate, loving, kind, and Christlike; we will be all the time growing in those graces. Now, we can tell whether we have that spirit or not. "If any one have not the spirit of Christ, he is none of His." Now, that is a sign that we have a good hope, and if we haven't got the Spirit of Christ, our hope is worthless.

Now, I was speaking about that house on the foundation. If you will turn to Isaiah, twenty-eighth chapter and sixteenth verse, you will find that the foundation is already laid. "Therefore; thus saith the Lord God. Behold, I lay in Zion for a foundation a stone, a tried stone, a precious corner stone, a sure foundation; he that believeth shall not make haste." There it is tried; it is a precious cornerstone; it is a sure foundation. It was tried when Christ was here. He is the chief cornerstone. He was tried. The Scribes tried Him. The Sadducees tried Him. He was tried by the law. He kept the law. He was tried by and He overcame death. He was tried by Satan. Satan came and presented temptation after temptation, and He said, "Get thee hence." He overcame Satan. He was tried by the grave, and He conquered the grave.

This stone has been tested and tried. Now, if we build on that, we have a sure foundation. There is none other name under heaven given among men whereby we must be saved. "There is no other foundation that man can lay than that is laid," and all who build on that foundation shall be saved. Let the storms come then and try that foundation. It has been tried. Your foundation, if you build on any other, has never been tested. It has not been tried. Your hope has not been tried. Our hope has. Because our hope is in Jesus Christ and was put to the test, we have a hope that is sure and firm if we are in Christ.

Now, a false hope just flatters people. It is a great flatterer. It makes people think they are all right when they are all wrong. Someone has said that false hopes are like spider webs. The maid comes in with a broom and sweeps them all down. When a storm comes, the foundation of our false hopes is all gone. Suppose death should come and look you in the face this afternoon and say to you, "This is your last day," and should begin to lay his cold, icy hand upon you, and you should begin to look around to see if you had got a foundation and a good hope. Would you be ready to meet God? That is the question.

Now, what may happen any day let us be ready for every day. You know very well there is not one of us but we may be summoned this very day into the presence of God. Do you have a hope that will stand the dying hour? Have you a hope that will stand the test? If you have not, you can give up your false hope today and get a good one, a hope that is worth having, that has been tried and tested.

There were two millers who used to take care of a mill. Every night at midnight the miller used to get into his boat from his house and go down the stream to the mill. He used to get out about two or three hundred yards above the dam and go to the mill. His brother miller would take the boat and row back to the house. One night this miller went down as usual at midnight and fell asleep and when he woke up found he was almost going over the dam, the water going over the dam having waked him. He realized in a moment his condition, that if he went over that dam it was sure death. He seized the oars and tried to row back, but the current was too strong, and he could not pull against it. But he managed in the darkness to get his boat near the shore, and he caught hold of a little twig. He went to pull himself out of the boat, and the twig began to give way at the roots. He looked all around and could find nothing else to get hold of; he could just hold on to the twig and keep his boat from going over the dam. If he pulled a little harder and tried to pull himself up, the little twig would give way; and he just cried then for help.

His hope was not a good one. He would perish if he let go and perish if he held on. He just cried at the top of his voice for help, and help came. They came and threw a rope over the cleft of the rock, and he let go of the twig and laid hold of the rope and was saved.

Those Who Have a Good Hope

I have come here to throw a rope over to you and to give you a good hope. Now, we have a hope here that is worth having. Let that false hope of yours go; you will perish if you will hold on to it. Let it go and lay hold of a hope that is set before you.

Now, you know that hope in Scripture never is used to express a doubt. When people say they hope they are Christians, it is not really proper. You cannot find any Christians in the Bible who say they *hope* they are Christians. It is something that has already taken place. We don't hope we are Christians. If a man asks me if I am a married man, I would not say I hope I am. That would cast a reflection on my marriage vows. If a man asks me if I am an American, I would not say I hope I am. I was born in this country. I am an American. I am not anything else. Now, if I have been born of God, born of the Spirit, and I contend it is our privilege to know, I don't say, "I hope I am a Christian." I know in Whom I have believed. I will tell you what hope is used for in Scripture. It is used to express our hope of the resurrection or the coming of the Lord Jesus Christ, something to take place. It is a sure hope. About every time that hope is used in Scripture, it is used either to express our hope of the resurrection or the coming back of our Lord and Master.

That is the blessed hope in Titus. We are waiting for our Lord and Master from heaven. We have not a doubt. It is a sure hope. And yet a great many people seem to think that hope here in the Bible is used to express a doubt. "We hope that we are Christians." We ought to know that we are His. We ought to know that we have passed from death unto life. We ought to know in Whom we have believed, that we are looking forward to the time when these vile bodies shall be raised incorruptible, when that which has been sown in weakness shall be raised with power. We are living in the glorious hope that when our dead shall come back again, the loved ones who are laid away in the cemeteries shall come when the Lord of heaven shall descend with a shout. "When the trump of God is heard, the dead in Christ shall rise first; then we which are alive and remain shall be caught up, together with them in the clouds, to meet the Lord in the air."

So we stand with our loins girded and our lights burning, waiting for the coming of the Master.

Now, it says here in Proverbs, "The hope of the righteous shall be gladness." "Happy is he that hath the God of Jacob for his hope, whose hope is in the Lord." It is not in some resolution that he has made; it is not in some act of his; it is not that he has joined some church; it is not that he reads his Bible or that he says his prayers. His expectation is from God; his hope is in God. Never was a man disappointed who put his hope in God. God will fulfill His word. There is no such thing as a man being disappointed who puts his hope in God. But the trouble is, you know, we are putting our hopes in one another, and we are being disappointed. We are putting our hopes in ourselves, and our treacherous hearts are disappointing us, and then we are cast down. But what we want is to put our hope in Him, not ourselves.

A well-grounded hope is good for all time. It is good in poverty. It is good in sickness. It is good in the dying hour; and when we lay a body down in the grave, we have a hope in its coming back again. We lay down with sure hope, a glorious hope. O, how hope cheers us! You know it was Hopeful (in Bunyan's *Pilgrim's Progress*) who came along and cheered Christian. That is what hope is for. We are looking forward to a blessed hope.

Now, there is a passage in the sixth chapter of Hebrews that I want to call to your attention: "That by two immutable things, in which it was impossible for God to lie, we might have a strong consolation, who had fled for refuge to lay hold upon the hope set before us; which hope we have as an anchor to the soul, both sure and steadfast, and which enters into that within the veil; whither the forerunner is for us entered, even Jesus, made an high priest forever after the order of Melchisedec." What the anchor is to the ship, hope is to the soul; as long as the anchor holds, the ship is perfectly safe.

Now, if I were to die this afternoon and were to give a reason for the hope that is within me, I will tell you where I would find it—not in my feelings, not in my resolutions, not that I joined the church twenty odd years ago. I believe it is all right to unite with the church and work for it. We ought to love the church; it is the dearest institution on earth. If I was going to die this afternoon, my faith would be right here, "Verily, verily, I say unto you, he that heareth my word, and believeth on Him that sent me, hath everlasting life, and shall not come into condemnation, but is passed from death unto life." Now, if I did not get eternal life by believing on the Lord Jesus Christ when I came to Him, what did I get? If eternal life is not the gift of God, what is it? Then, if we have eternal life, we have something that cannot perish. It is a life that carries me beyond the grave, that reaches away over on to resurrection ground, that carries me on and on forever. The wages of sin is death, but the gift of God is eternal life. Eternal life is a gift, and I just took it. That is my hope. I don't want any other hope. If I had to die today, I could just pillow my dying head upon the truth of that verse and rest it there.

A man said to me the other day, "How do you feel?" I said, "It has been so long since I have thought of myself, I don't know; I would have to stop to think it over."

I thank God my salvation doesn't rest upon my feelings. I thank God my hope is not centered in my feelings. If it was, it would be a very treacherous thing. I would be very hopeful one day and cast down the next day. I would not give much for a hope that is anchored in my feelings. I would not give much for a hope that is based upon my treacherous heart. But I tell you that a hope that is based upon Jesus Christ's Word is a hope worth having. Now, He said it; let us believe it; let us lay hold of it by faith. "Verily, verily," which means "truly, truly," "he that heareth my word"—I have heard it. Satan can't make me believe that I have not. I have read it; I have handled it— "He that heareth my word and believeth on Him that sent Me hath everlasting life."

It doesn't say that you shall have it when you come to die, but you can have it right here this afternoon before you go out of this church. That is a hope worth having, isn't it? "Hath everlasting life, and shall not come into condemnation," which means "into judgment," but "is passed from death unto life." There is my hope. I have stood there for twenty odd years. I have been assailed by doubts. I have been assailed by unbelief. I have been attacked by the enemy of all righteousness; I tell you for twenty odd years I have been able to stand fair and square right on that rock. God said it. I believe it; God said it. I lay hold of it, and I just rest right there. What we want is to let our hope go down like an anchor into the Word of God, and that gives us something to rest upon.

A great many people are waiting for some feeling. I will venture to say that more than half of this audience has come here today and taken their seats in the hope that something will be said that shall impress them. You say, "I hope that man will say something that will impress me." You are waiting for some impression, something to strike you. There is a man up in my native town, now fifty-eight years old, with whom I have talked I don't know how many times, and every time I talk to him he says, "Well, it hasn't struck me yet." "What do you mean?" "Well," he says, "it hasn't struck me yet." "Well," I said, "that is a queer expression. What do you mean?" He would come out to meetings and wait through the meeting for something to strike him. "What do you mean?" "Well, I say it hasn't struck me yet."

You laugh at it, but that is yourself. You need not laugh at yourself. You will find the church is full of people who are waiting for something to strike them. What we want is to take God's Word and let the feelings take care of themselves. God said it. I will believe it, and I will rest my soul upon the Word of God, not upon my feelings.

Just take another word, "He came unto His own, and His own received Him not; but to as many as received Him, to them gave He power to become the sons of God, even to them that believe on His name." To as many as received Him. It is not dogma; it is not creed; it is not doctrine; it is not feeling; it is not an impression; it is a person. "As many as received Him, to them gave He power to become the sons of God." We get power to serve God, power to live for God, power to work for God by receiving Christ, and there is no power until we do receive Him. What we want is to receive God's gift to the world. When He gave up Christ, He gave all He had. He literally emptied heaven. And He wants you to take Christ as you would take any other gift and receive it. Lay hold of that gift, and it will give you hope, and if you should, inside of twenty-four hours you can say, "The anchor holds; I have a hope."

If God said if I would receive His Son, He would give me power to receive Him. I trust Him and that is all He asks us to do. Let not anyone here today say he can't believe on the Lord Jesus Christ. You have the power if you will. The will is the key to the human heart. "Ye will not come unto Me that ye might have life." You will not come unto Me and get this good hope. You can have it. Take it. God offers it to you. You can lay hold of this hope today. You can become His if you will.

NOTES

The Happy Hope

Alexander MacLaren (1826–1910) was one of Great Britain's most famous preachers. While pastoring the Union Chapel, Manchester (1858–1903), he became known as "the prince of expository preachers." Rarely active in denominational or civic affairs, MacLaren invested his time in studying the Word in the original languages and sharing its truths with others in sermons that are still models of effective expository preaching. He published a number of books of sermons and climaxed his ministry by publishing his monumental *Expositions of Holy Scripture.*

This message is taken from *Sermons Preached in Manchester,* third series, published in 1902 by Funk and Wagnalls Company.

Alexander MacLaren

6

THE HAPPY HOPE

Look for that blessed hope, and the glorious appearing of the great God and our Savior Jesus Christ (Titus 2:13).

THERE ARE TWO appearances spoken of in this context—the appearance of "the grace of God that bringeth salvation" and parallel with that, though at the same time contrasted with it as being in very important senses one in nature and principle though diverse in purpose and diverse in manner, is what the Apostle here calls "the glorious appearing of the great God."

The antithesis of contrast and of parallel is still more striking in the original than in our version, where our translators have adopted a method of rendering of which they are very fond and which very often obscures the full meaning of the text. Paul wrote, "Looking for that blessed (or "happy") hope, even *the appearing of the glory* of the great God and our Savior," where you see he contrasts, even more sharply than our Bible makes him do, the past appearance of the grace and the future appearance of the glory.

Then, further, "this appearance of the glory," however bright with the terrible beauty and flashing luster of Divine majesty it may be, seems to the Apostle to be infinitely desirable and becomes to him a happy hope. The reality, when it comes, will be pure joy. The irradiation of its approach shines from afar on his brightening face and lightens his heart with a hope which is a prophetic joy. And the attitude of the Christian soul toward it is to be that of glad expectation, watching the dawning east and ready to salute the sun.

And yet further, this attitude of happy expectation of the glory is one chief object to be attained by the grace that has appeared. It came "teaching," or rather (as the word more accurately means) "disciplining, that we should live looking for that happy hope."

So then, we have here for our consideration three points embodied in these words—The grace of God has appeared, the glory of God is to appear; the appearance of the glory is a blessed hope; the disciplining of the grace prepares us for the expectation of the glory.

Grace and Glory

First, then, take that thought—The appearance of the grace leads to the appearance of the glory.

The identity of the form of expression in the two clauses is intended to suggest the *likeness* of and the *connection* between the two appearances. In both there is a visible manifestation of God, and the latter rests upon the former and completes and crowns it

But the *difference* between the two is as strongly marked as the analogy; and it is not difficult to grasp distinctly the difference which the Apostle intends. While both are manifestations of the Divine character in exercise, the specific phase (so to speak) of that character which appears is in one case "grace" and in the other "glory." If one might venture on any illustration in regard to such a subject, it is as when the pure white light is sent through glass of different colors and at one moment beams mild through refreshing green and at the next flames in fiery red that warns of danger.

The two words which are pitted against each other here have each a very wide range of meaning. But, as employed in this place, their antithetical force is clear enough. "Grace" is active love exercised toward inferiors and toward those who deserve something else. So the grace of God is the active energy of His love which stoops from the throne to move among men and, departing from the strict ground of justice and retribution, deals with us not according to our sins nor rewards us according to our iniquities.

And then the contrasted word "glory" has not only a very wide meaning but also a definite and specific force which the very antithesis suggests. The "glory of God," I believe, in one very important sense is His "grace." The highest glory of God is the exhibition of forgiving and long-suffering love. Nothing can be grander! Nothing can be more majestic! Nothing, in the very profoundest sense of the word, can be more truly Divine—more lustrous with all the beams of manifest Deity than the gentle raying forth of His mercy and His goodness!

But then, while that is the profoundest thought of the glory of God, there is another truth to be taken in conjunction with it. The phrase has in Scripture a well marked and distinct sense which may be illustrated from the Old Testament, where it generally means not so much the total impression of majesty and power made upon men by the whole revealed Divine character, but rather the visible light which shone between the Cherubim and proclaimed the present God. Connected with this more limited sense is the wider one of that which the material light above the mercy seat symbolized— and which we have no better words to describe than to call it the Ineffable and Inaccessible Brightness of that awful Name.

The contrast between the two will be suggested by a passage to which I may refer. The ancient lawgiver said, "I beseech thee show me thy glory." The answer was, "I will make all my goodness pass before thee." The eye of man is incapable of apprehending the uncreated divine lustrousness and splendor of light but capable of receiving some dim and partial apprehensions of the goodness, not indeed in its fullness but in its consequences. And that goodness, though it be the brightest of "the glories that compose his name," is not the only possible nor the only actual manifestation of the glory of God. The prayer was unfulfilled when offered; for to answer it, as is possible for earth, would have been to antedate the slow evolution of the counsels of God. But answered it will be and that on this globe. "Every eye shall see him."

The grace has appeared when Divine Love is incarnate among us. The long-suffering gentleness we have seen. And in it we have seen, in a very real sense, the glory, for "we beheld his *glory*—full of *grace*." But beyond that lies ready to be revealed in the last time the glory, the lustrous light, the majestic splendor, the flaming fire of manifest Divinity.

Again, the two verses thus bracketed together and brought into sharp contrast also suggest how like as well as how unlike these manifestations are to be.

In both cases there is an appearance in the strictest sense of the word, that is to say, a thing visible to men's senses. Can we see the grace of God? We can see the love in exercise, cannot we? How? "He that hath seen me hath seen the Father; and how sayest thou then, Shew us the Father?" The appearance of Christ was the making visible in human form of the love of God!

My brother, the appearance of the glory will be the same—the making visible in human form of the light of throned and sovereign Deity. The one was incarnation; the other will be incarnation. The one was patent to men's senses—so will the other be. The grace has appeared. The glory *is* to appear. "Why stand ye gazing up into heaven? This same Jesus shall so come in like manner as ye have seen him go." An historical fact, a bodily visibility, a manifestation of the Divine nature and character in human form upon earth and living and moving amongst men! As "Christ was once offered to bear the sins of many," so "unto them that look for him shall he appear the second time without sin unto salvation." The two are strictly parallel. As the grace was visible in action by a man among men, so the glory will be. What we look for is an actual bodily manifestation in a human form on the solid earth of the glory of God!

And then I would notice how emphatically this idea of the glory being all sphered and embodied in the living person of Jesus Christ proclaims His Divine nature. It is "the appearance of the glory"—then mark the next words— "of the great God and our Savior."

I am not going to enter upon the question of the interpretation of these words which by many very competent authorities have been taken as all referring to Jesus Christ and as being a singular instance in Scripture of the attribution to Him directly and without any explanation or modification of the name "the great God!" I do not think that either grammar or dogma require that interpretation here. But I think that if we take the words to refer distinctly to the Father and to the Son, the inference as to Christ's true and proper divinity which comes from them, so understood, is no less strong than the other interpretation would make it. For in that case, the same one and indissoluble glory is ascribed to God the Father and to Christ our Lord, and the same act is the appearance of both.

The Human possesses the Divine glory in such reality and fullness as it would be insanity if it were not blasphemy and blasphemy if it were not absurdity to predicate of any simple man. The words coincide with His own saying, "The Son of Man shall come in *his glory and of the Father*," and point us necessarily and inevitably to the wonderful thought that the glory of God is capable of being fully imparted to, possessed by, and revealed through Jesus Christ; that the glory of God is Christ's glory, and the glory of Christ is God's. In deep, mysterious, real, eternal union the Father and the Son, the light and the ray, the fountain and the source, pour themselves out in loving-kindness on the world and shall flash themselves in splendor at the last when the Son of Man "shall be manifested in his own glory and of the Father!"

And, then, I must touch very briefly another remarkable and plain contrast indicated in our text between these two "appearings." They are not only unlike in the subject (so to speak) or substance of the manifestation, but also in the purpose. The grace comes, patient, gentle, sedulous, laboring for our training and discipline. The glory comes—there is no word of training there!

What does the glory come for? The one rises upon a benighted world—lambent and lustrous and gentle, like the slow, silent, climbing of the silvery moon through the darkling sky. But the other blazes out with a leap upon a stormy heaven—"as the lightning cometh out of the east, and shineth even unto the west," writing its fierce message across all the black page of the sky in one instant, "so shall also the coming of the Son of Man be." Like some patient mother, the "grace of God has moved amongst men," with entreaty, with loving rebuke, with loving chastisement.

She has been counselor and comforter. She has disciplined and fostered with more than maternal wisdom and love. "Her ways are ways of pleasantness, and all her paths are peace." But the glory appears for another purpose and in another guise—"Who is this that cometh with dyed garments? I that speak in righteousness, mighty to save. Wherefore *art thou* red in thine apparel? I have trodden the winepress alone—for the day of vengeance is in mine heart, and the year of my redeemed is come."

Glory and Hope

But we have now to look at the second thought which is involved in these words, and that is, *The appearing of the glory is a blessed hope.*

The hope is blessed, or as we have already remarked, the word "happy" may, perhaps, be substituted with advantage. Because it will be full of blessedness when it is a reality, therefore it is full of joy while it is but a hope.

The characteristics of that future manifestation of glory are not such that its coming is wholly and universally a joy. There is something terrible in the beauty, something menacing in the brightness. But it is worth noticing that notwithstanding all that gathers about it of terror, all that gathers about it of awful splendor, all that is solemn and heart-shaking in the thought of judgment and retribution for the past, the irreversible and irrevocable past, yet to Paul it was the very crown of all his expectations of and the very shining summit of all his desires for the future—that Christ should appear.

The ancient church thought a great deal more about the coming of Jesus Christ than about death—thought a great deal more about His coming than about heaven. To them the future was not so much a time of rest for themselves as the manifestation of their Lord. To them the way of passing out of life was not so much seeing corruption as being caught up together in the air.

And how far the darkness, which our Lord declared to be the Divine counsel in regard to that future coming, enwrapped even those who upon all other points received the Divine inspiration which made and makes them forevermore the infallible teachers and authorities for the Christian Church is a moot question. If it were certain that the Apostle expected Christ's coming during his own lifetime, I do not know that we need be troubled at that as if it shook his authority, seeing that almost the last words which Christ spoke to His Apostles were a distinct declaration that He had not to reveal to them and they were not to know "the times and the seasons which the Father has put in his own power," and seeing that the office of that Holy Spirit, as whose organs Paul and the other writers of the New Testament are our authoritative teachers, is expressly declared to be the bringing all things to their remembrance, whatsoever Christ had revealed. If, then, He expressly excepts from the compass of His revelation this point, it can be no derogation from the completeness of an inspired writer's authority if he knows it not.

And if one takes into account the whole of Paul's words on the subject, they seem to express rather the same double anticipation which we too have to cherish, desiring and looking on the one hand for the Savior from heaven, desiring on the other hand to depart and be with Christ which is far better. The numerous places in which Paul speaks of his own decease, sometimes as longed for, sometimes as certain, and, latterly, as near, are inconsistent with the theory that he looked for Christ's coming as certain in his own lifetime. So, too, are other anticipations which he expresses as to the future course of the church and progress of the Gospel in the world. He, like us, would appear to have had before his expectations the alternative. He knew not when the glory might burst upon the world, therefore he was ever standing as one who waits for his Lord. He knew not when he might have to die, therefore he labored that, "whether present or absent, he might be pleasing to him."

But that is not the point upon which I want to say a word. Dear brethren, the hope is a *happy* one. If we know "the grace," we shall not be afraid of "the glory." If the grace has disciplined in any measure, we may be sure that we shall partake in its perfection. They who have seen the face of Christ looking down as it were upon them from the midst of the great darkness of the cross and beneath the crown of thorns need not be afraid to see the same face looking down upon them from amidst all the blaze of the light and from beneath the many crowns of the kingdoms of the world and the royalties of the heavens. Whosoever has learned to love and believe in the manifestation of the grace, he, and he only, can believe and hope for the manifestation of the glory.

And, Christian men and women, while thus the one ground upon which that assurance, "The Lord cometh," can be anything to us except a dread, if it is a belief at all, is the simple reliance upon His past work—let me urge the further consideration upon you and myself, how shamefully all of us neglect and overlook that blessed expectation! *We* live by hope. God, indeed, is above all hope. To that infinite eye before which all things that were and are and are to come lie open and manifest, or rather are insphered in His own person and self, to Him who is the living past, the abiding present, the present future, there is no expectation. The animal creation is below hope. But for us who live on the central level— half-way between a beast and God, if I may say so—for us our lives are tossed about between memory and expectation.

We all of us possess and most of us prostitute that wonderful gift—of shaping out some conception of the future. And what do we do with it? It might knit us to God, bear us up amid the glories of the abysses of the skies. We use it for making to ourselves pictures of fools' paradises of present pleasures or of successful earthly joys. The folly of men is not that they live by hope but that they set their hopes on such things—

> They build too low
> Who build beneath the stars!

As for every other part of human nature, so for this strange faculty of our being the Gospel points to its true object, and the Gospel gives its only consecration. Dear brethren, is it true of us that into our hearts there steals subtle, impalpable, but quickening as the land breeze laden with the fragrance of flowers to the sailor tossing on the barren sea, a hidden but yet mighty hope of an inheritance with Him—when He shall appear? With eye lifted above and fixed upon the heavens do I look beyond the clouds into the stars? Alas! alas the world drives that hope out of our hearts. It is with us as with the people in some rude country fair and scene of riot where the booths and the shows and the drinking-places are pitched upon the edge of the common, and one step from the braying of the trumpets brings you into the solemn stillness of the night, and high above the stinking flare of the oil lamps there is the pure light of the stars in the sky, and not one amongst the many clowns that are stumbling about in the midst of sensual dissipation ever looks up to see that calm home that is arched above them!

We live for the present, do we not? And there, if only we would lift our eyes, there, even now, is the sign of the Son of Man in the heavens. My friend, it is as much an element of a Christian's character and a part of his plain imperative duty to look for His appearing as it is to live "soberly, righteously, and godly in this present world!"

Grace as a Discipline

Well then, finally, one word about the last consideration here, namely, *The grace disciplines us to hope for the glory.*

The very idea of discipline involves the notion that it is a preparatory stage, a transient process for a permanent result. It carries with it the idea of immaturity, of apprenticeship, so to speak. If it is discipline, it is discipline for some condition which is not yet reached. And so, if the grace of God comes "disciplining," then there must be something beyond the epoch and era within which the discipline is confined.

And that just runs out into two considerations upon which I have not time to dwell. Take the characteristics of the grace—clearly enough, it is preparing men for something beyond itself. Yield to the discipline and the hope will grow.

Take the characteristics of the grace. Here is a great system based upon a stupendous and inconceivable act of Divine sacrifice involving a mysterious identification of the whole race of sinful men with the Savior, embodying the most wonderful love of God, and being the propitiation for the sins of the whole world. Here is a life perfectly innocent, perfectly pure, brought to the extremity of evil, and having never swerved one inch from the Divine commandments, yet dying at last under a consciousness of separation and desertion from God. Here is a cross, a resurrection, an ascension, an omnipotent Spirit, an all-guiding Word, a whole series of powers and agencies brought to bear! Does anyone believe that such a wealth of Divine energy and resource would be put forth and employed for purposes that break short off when a man is put into his coffin and that have nothing beyond this world for their field?

Here is a perfect instrument for making people perfect, and what does it do? It makes them so good and leaves them so bad that unless they are to be made still better and perfected, God's work on the soul is at once an unparalleled success and a confounding failure—a puzzle in that having done so much it does not do more, in that having done so little it has done so much. The achievements of Christianity upon single souls and its failures upon those for whom it has done most, when measured against and compared with its manifest adaptation to a loftier issue than it has ever reached here on earth, all coincide to say the grace—because its purpose is discipline and because its purpose is but partially achieved here on earth—demands a glory when they whose darkness has been partially made "light in the Lord" by the discipline of grace shall "blaze forth as the sun" in the Heavenly Father's Kingdom of Glory.

Yield to the discipline, and the hope will be strengthened. You will never entertain in any vigor and operative power upon your lives the expectation of that coming of the glory unless you live soberly, righteously, and godly in this present world.

That discipline submitted to is, if I may say so, like that great apparatus which you find by the side of an astronomer's biggest telescope to wheel it upon its center and to point its tube to the star on which he would look. So our anticipation and desire, the faculty of expectation which we have, is wont to be directed along the low level of earth, and it needs the pinions and levers of that gracious discipline, making us sober, righteous, godly, in order to heave it upward, full-front against the sky, that the stars may shine into it.

The speculum, the object-glass, must be polished and cut by many a stroke and much friction ere it will reflect "the image of the heavenly"; so grace disciplines us patiently, slowly, by repeated strokes, by much rubbing, by much pain—disciplines us to live in self-restraint, in righteousness and godliness, and then the cleared eye beholds the heavens, and the purged heart grows toward "the coming" as its hope and its life.

Dear brethren, let us not fling away the treasures of our hearts' desires upon trifles and earth. Let us not "set our hopes on that which is not" nor paint that misty wall that rings round our present with evanescent colors like the landscapes of a dream. We may have a hope which is a certainty as sure as a history, as vivid as present fact. Let us love and trust to Him who has been manifested to save us from our sins and in whom we behold all the grace and truth of God. If our eyes have learned to behold and our hearts to love Him whom we have not seen amid all the bewildering glares and false appearances of the present, our hopes will happily discern Him and be at rest amid the splendors of that solemn hour when He shall come in His glory to render to every man according to His works.

With that hope the future, near or far, has no fears hidden in its depths. Without it, there is no real anchorage for our trembling hearts and nothing to hold by when the storm comes. The alternative is before each of us, "having *no* hope," or "looking for that blessed hope." God help us all to believe that Christ *has* come for me! Then I shall be glad when I think that Christ will come again to receive me unto Himself!

Hope Perfectly

Alexander MacLaren (1826–1910) was one of Great Britain's most famous preachers. While pastoring the Union Chapel, Manchester (1858–1903), he became known as "the prince of expository preachers." Rarely active in denominational or civic affairs, MacLaren invested his time in studying the Word in the original languages and sharing its truths with others in sermons that are still models of effective expository preaching. He published a number of books of sermons and climaxed his ministry by publishing his monumental *Expositions of Holy Scripture*.

This message is taken from *Expositions of Holy Scripture*, volume 16.

Alexander MacLaren

7

HOPE PERFECTLY

> Wherefore, gird up the loins of your mind, be sober, and
> hope to the end, for the grace that is to be brought unto
> you at the revelation of Jesus Christ (1 Peter 1:13).

CHRISTIANITY HAS transformed hope and given it a new
importance by opening to it a new world to move in and
supplying to it new guarantees to rest on. There is something very remarkable in the prominence given to hope in
the New Testament and in the power ascribed to it to
order a noble life. Paul goes so far as to say that we are
saved by it. To a Christian it is no longer a pleasant
dream which may be all an illusion, indulgence in which
is pretty sure to sap a man's force, but it is a certain
anticipation of certainties, the effect of which will be increased energy and purity. So our Apostle, having in the
preceding context in effect summed up the whole Gospel,
bases upon that summary a series of exhortations, the
transition to which is marked by the "wherefore" at the
beginning of my text. The application of that word is to be
extended so as to include all that has preceded in the
letter, and there follows a series of practical advises, the
first of which, the grace or virtue which he puts in the
forefront of everything, is not what you might have expected, but it is "hope perfectly."

I may just remark before going further in reference to
the language of my text, that, accurately translated, the
two exhortations which precede that *to hope* are subsid-
iary to it, for we ought to read, "Wherefore, girding up the
loins of your mind, and being sober, hope." That is to say,
these two are preliminaries or conditions or means by
which the desired perfecting of the Christian hope is to be
sought and attained.

Another preliminary remark which I must make is that

what is enjoined here has not reference to the duration but to the quality of the Christian hope. It is not "to the end," but as the Margin of the Authorized and the Revised Version concurs in saying, it is "hope perfectly."

So, then, there are three things here—the object, the duty, and the cultivation of Christian hope. Let us take these three things in order.

I. The Object of Christian Hope

Now that is stated in somewhat remarkable language as "the grace that is to be brought unto you at the revelation of Jesus Christ." We generally use that word "grace" with a restricted signification to the gifts of God to men here on earth. It is the earnest of the inheritance, rather than its fullness. But here it is quite obvious that by the expression the Apostle means the very same thing as he has previously designated in the preceding context by three different phrases—"an inheritance incorruptible and undefiled," "praise and honor and glory at the revelation of Jesus Christ," and "the end of your faith, even the salvation of your souls." The "grace" is not contrasted with the "glory" but is another name for the glory. It is not the earnest of the inheritance, but it is the inheritance itself. It is not the means toward attaining the progressive and finally complete "salvation of your souls," but it is that complete salvation in all its fullness.

Now, that is an unusual use of the word, but that it should be employed here, as describing the future great object of the Christian hope, suggests two or three thoughts. One is that that ultimate blessedness with all its dim, nebulous glories which can only be resolved into their separate stars when we are millions of leagues nearer to its luster is like the faintest glimmer of a new and better life in a soul here on earth, purely and solely the result of the undeserved, condescending love of God that stoops to sinful men and instead of retribution bestows upon them a heaven.

The grace that saved us at first, the grace that comes to us filtered in drops during our earthly experience is poured upon us in a flood at last. And the brightest glory of heaven is as much a manifestation of the divine grace as the first rudimentary germs of a better life now and here. The foundation, the courses of the building, the glittering pinnacle on the summit with its golden spire reaching still higher into the blue is all the work of the same unmerited, stooping, pardoning love. Glory is grace, and heaven is the result of God's pardoning mercy.

There is another suggestion here to be made, springing from this eloquent use of this term, and that is not merely the identity of the source of the Christian experience upon earth and in the future, but the identity of that Christian experience itself in regard of its essential character. If I may say so, it is all of a piece, homogeneous, and of one web. The robe is without seam, woven throughout of the same thread. The life of the humblest Christian, the most imperfect Christian, the most infantile Christian, the most ignorant Christian here on earth has for its essential characteristics the very same things as the lives of the strong spirits that move in light around the throne and receive into their expanding nature the ever-increasing fullness of the glory of the Lord. Grace here is glory in the bud; glory yonder is grace in the fruit.

But there is still further to be noticed another great thought that comes out of this remarkable language. The words of my text, literally rendered, are "the grace that is being brought unto you." Now, there have been many explanations of that remarkable phrase which I think is not altogether exhausted by nor quite equivalent to that which represents it in our version—namely, "to be brought unto you." That relegates it all into the future; but in Peter's conception it is in some sense in the present. It is "being brought."

What does that mean? There are far-off stars in the sky, the beams from which have set out from their home of light millenniums since and have been rushing through the waste places of the universe since long before men were, and they have not reached our eyes yet. But they are on the road. And so in Peter's conception, the apocalypse of glory which is the crowning manifestation of grace is rushing toward us through the ages, through the spheres, and it will be here some day, and the beams will strike upon our faces and make them glow with its light. So certain is the arrival of the grace that the Apostle deals with it as already on its way. The great thing on which the Christian hope fastens is no "peradventure" but a good which has already begun to journey toward us.

Again, there is another thought still to be suggested, and that is, the revelation of Jesus Christ is the coming to His children of this grace which is glory, of this glory which is grace. For mark how the Apostle says, "the grace which is being brought to you in the revelation of Jesus Christ." And that revelation to which he here refers is not the past one in His incarnate life upon earth, but it is the future one to which the hope of the faithful church ought ever to be steadfastly turned, the correlated truth to that other one on which its faith rests. On these two great pillars rising like columns on either side of the gulf of time, "He has come," "He will come," the bridge is suspended by which we may safely pass over the foaming torrent that else would swallow us up. The revelation in the past cries out for the revelation in the future. The Cross demands the throne. That He has come once, a sacrifice for sin, stands incomplete, like some building left unfinished with tugged stones protruding which prophesy an addition at a future day, unless you can add "unto them that look for Him will He appear the second time without sin unto salvation." In that revelation of Jesus Christ His children shall find the glory-grace which is the object of their hope.

So say all the New Testament writers. "When Christ, who is our life, shall appear, then shall we also appear with Him in glory," says Paul. "The grace that is to be brought unto you in the revelation of Jesus Christ," chimes in Peter. And John completes the trio with his "We know that when He shall appear we shall be like Him." These three things, brethren—with Christ, glory with Him, likeness to Him—are all that we know, and blessed be God! all that we need to know of that dim future. And the more we confine ourselves to these triple great certainties and sweep aside all subordinate matters which are concealed partly because they could not be revealed and partly because they would not help us if we knew them, the better for the simplicity and the power and the certainty of our hope. The object of Christian hope is Christ in His revelation, in His presence, in His communication to us for glory, in His assimilating of us to Himself.

> It is enough that Christ knows all,
> And we shall be with Him.

"The grace that is being brought unto you in the revelation of Jesus Christ."

II. The Duty of the Christian Hope

And now notice the duty of the Christian hope. Hope a duty? That strikes one as somewhat strange. I very much doubt whether the ordinary run of good people do recognize it as being as imperative a duty for them to cultivate hope as to cultivate any other Christian excellence or virtue. For one man who sets himself deliberately and consciously to brighten up and to make more operative in his daily life the hope of future blessedness, you will find a hundred that set themselves to other kinds of perfecting of their Christian character. And yet, surely, there do not need any words to enforce the fact that this hope full of immortality is no mere luxury which a Christian may add to the plain fare of daily duty or leave untasted according as he likes, but that it is an indispensable element in all vigorous and life-dominating Christian experience.

I do not need to dwell upon that, except just to suggest that such a vividness and continuity of calm anticipation of a certain good beyond the grave is one of the strongest of all motives to the general robustness and efficacy of a Christian life. People used to say a few years ago a great deal more than they do now that the Christian expectation of heaven was apt to weaken energy upon earth, and they used to sneer at us and talk about our "other worldliness" as if it were a kind of weakness and defect attached to the Christian experience. They have pretty well given that up now. Anti-Christian sarcasm like everything else has its fashions, and other words of reproach and contumely have now taken the place of that.

The plain fact is that no one sees the greatness of the present unless he regards it as being the vestibule of the future and that this present life is unintelligible and insignificant unless beyond it and led up to by it and shaped through it there lies the eternal life beyond. The low, flat plain is dreary and desolate, featureless and melancholy when the sky above it is filled with clouds. But sweep away the cloud-rack and let the blue arch itself above the brown moorland, and all glows into luster, and every undulation is brought out, and tiny shy forms of beauty are found in every corner.

And so if you drape heaven with the clouds and mists born of indifference and worldliness, the world becomes mean, but if you dissipate the cloud and unveil heaven, earth is greatened. If the hope of the grave that is to be brought unto you at the revelation of Jesus Christ shines out above all the flatness of earth, then life becomes solemn, noble, worthy of, demanding, and rewarding our most strenuous efforts. No man can and no man will strike such effectual blows on things present as the man, the strength of whose arm is derived from the conviction that every stroke of the hammer on things present is shaping that which will abide with him forever.

My text not only enjoins this hope as a duty but also enjoins the perfection of it as being a thing to be aimed at by all Christian people. What is the perfection of hope? Two qualities, certainty and continuity. Certainty; the definition of earthly hope is an anticipation of good less than certain, and so in all the operations of this great faculty which are limited within the range of earth, you get blended as an indistinguishable throng, "hopes and fears that kindle hope," and that too often kill it. But the Christian has a certain anticipation of certain good, and to him memory may be no more fixed than hope, and the past no more unalterable and uncertain than the future.

The motto of our hope is not the "perhaps" which is the most that it can say when it speaks the tongue of earth, but the "verily! verily!" which comes to its enfranchised lips when it speaks the tongue of heaven. Your hope, oh Christian, should not be the tremulous thing that it often is which expresses itself in phrases like "Well! I do not know, but I tremblingly hope," but it should say, "I know and am sure of the rest that remaineth, not because of what I am but because of what He is."

Another element in the perfection of hope is its continuity. That hits home to us all, does it not? Sometimes in calm weather we catch a sight of the gleaming battlements of "the City which hath foundations," away across the sea, and then mists and driving storms come up and hide it.

There is a great mountain in Central Africa which if a man wishes to see, he must seize a fortunate hour in the early morning, for all the rest of the day it is swathed in clouds, invisible. Is that like your hope, Christian man and woman, gleaming out now and then and then again swallowed up in the darkness? Brethren! these two things, *certainty* and *continuity*, are possible for us. Alas! that they are so seldom enjoyed by us.

III. Cultivation of This Christian Hope

And now one last word. My text speaks about the discipline or cultivation of this Christian hope. It prescribes two things as auxiliary thereto. The way to cultivate the perfect hope which alone corresponds to the gift of God is "girding up the loins of your mind, and being sober." Of course, there is here one of the very few reminiscences that we have in the Epistles of the *ipsissima verba* of our Lord. Peter is evidently referring to our Lord's commandment to have "the loins girt and the lamps burning, and ye yourselves like unto men that wait for their Lord." I do not need to remind you of the Eastern dress that makes the metaphor remarkably significant, the loose robes that tangle a man's feet when he runs, that need to be girded up and belted tight around his waist as preliminary to all travel or toil of any kind. The metaphor is the same as that in our colloquial speech when we talk about a man "pulling himself together."

Just as an English workman will draw his belt a hole tighter when he has some special task to do, so Peter says to us, make a definite effort with resolute bracing up and concentration of all your powers, or you will never see the grace that is hurrying toward you through the centuries. There are abundance of loose, slack-braced people up and down the world in all departments, and they never come to any good.

It is a shame that any one should have his thoughts so loosely girt and vagrant as that any briar by the roadside can catch them and hinder his advance. But it is a tenfold shame for Christian people, with such an object to gaze upon, that they should let their minds be dissipated all over the trivialities of time and not gather them together and project them, as I may say, with all their force toward the sovereign realities of Eternity. A sixpence held close to your eye will blot out the sun, and the trifles of earth close to us will prevent us from realizing the things which neither sight, nor experience, nor testimony reveal to us, unless with clenched teeth, so to speak, we make dogged effort to keep them in mind.

The other preliminary and condition is "being sober" which, of course, you have to extend to its widest possible signification, implying not merely abstinence from or moderate use of intoxicants or material good for the appetites, but also the withdrawing of one's self sometimes wholly from and always restraining one's self in the use of the present and the material. A man has only a given definite quantity of emotion and interest to expend, and if he flings it all away on the world, he has none left for heaven. He will be like the miller who spoils some fair river by diverting its waters into his own sluice in order that he may grind some corn. If you have the faintest film of dust on the glass of the telescope or on its mirror, if it is a reflecting one, you will not see the constellations in the heavens; and if we have drawn over our spirits the film of earthly absorption, all these bright glories above will, so far as we are concerned, cease to be.

So, beloved, there is a solemn responsibility laid upon us by the gift of that great faculty of looking before and after. What did God make you and me capable of anticipating the future for? That we might let our hopes run along the low levels or that we might elevate them and twine them round the very pillars of God's Throne; which? I do not find fault with you because you hope but because you hope so meanly and about such trivial and transitory things.

I remember I once saw a seabird kept in a garden, confined within high walls and with clipped wings, set to pick up grubs and insects. It ought to have been away out, hovering over the free ocean, or soaring with sunlit wing to a height where earth became a speck and all its noises were hushed. That is what some of you are doing with your hope, degrading it to earth instead of letting it rise to God; enter within the veil and gaze upon the glory of the "inheritance incorruptible and undefiled."

Hope

George Campbell Morgan (1863–1945) was the son of
a British Baptist preacher and preached his first sermon
when he was 13 years old. He had no formal training for
the ministry, but his tireless devotion to the study of the
Bible helped him to become one of the leading Bible teachers of his day. Rejected by the Methodists, he was ordained into the Congregational ministry. He was associated
with Dwight L. Moody in the Northfield Bible conferences
and as an itinerant Bible teacher. He is best known as
the pastor of the Westminster Chapel, London (1904–17
and 1933–45). During his second term there, he had Dr.
D. Martyn Lloyd-Jones as his associate.

Morgan published more than sixty books and booklets,
and his sermons are found in *The Westminster Pulpit*
(Pickering and Inglis Ltd., London, 1906–1916). This sermon is from volume 8.

George Campbell Morgan

8

HOPE

By hope were we saved (Romans 8:24).

THE EXPERIENCE of hope is that of triumph over conditions and circumstances which are calculated to produce despair. Where there is no place for despair, there is none for hope. If there is no danger of despair, there is no possibility or necessity for hope. The old English word "hope" in all its mutations has retained the sense of expectation, of something desired and not yet attained. The Greek word of which it is a translation in my text, coming to us as it does from a primitive word meaning anticipation and almost always anticipation with pleasure, has exactly the same significance. Indeed, the word is used in the New Testament invariably in the sense of anticipation with pleasure and in the sense of desire. When that which is anticipated is realized, there is room neither for despair nor hope; when faith is lost to sight, then hope in full fruition dies; or, as the writer of this letter says in immediate connection with my text, "Hope that is seen is not hope; for who hopeth for that which he seeth?" This, then, is peculiarly a word for days of stress and strain.

Hope comes to its brightest shining in the presence of the deepest darkness. The function of hope is conditioned by the prevalence of conditions making for despair. We need not enter into any lengthy consideration of the distinction between faith and hope. Hope is an aspect of faith. According to the Biblical presentation of faith, it will be perfectly safe to say that the soul of man, looking upward in faith, is conscious of perfect confidence; that the soul of man, looking onward in faith, is conscious of hope; that the soul, looking around in faith, is conscious of peace. Faith is an attitude of the soul; hope is the experience which that attitude creates with regard to the future.

The apostolic declaration is made in connection with an argument in the course of which conditions calculated to produce despair were most clearly recognized and, indeed, described. The whole passage is one in which, in broad statement, the Apostle recognizes those things which persist until this hour: the trouble, the turmoil, the travail, the groaning of the world. "The whole creation groaneth and travaileth in pain together; . . . we ourselves groan within ourselves; . . . the Spirit Himself maketh intercession for us with groanings which cannot be uttered."

The way in which hope saves will best be apprehended if we consider, first, the nature of the hope which is referred to by the Apostle; second, the foundation of that hope; and, third, the effects which that hope produces.

The Nature of This Hope

If we are to understand the nature of the hope referred to, we must begin by a yet more careful examination of the need for this ministry of hope. It is important that we recognize that it is discovered in the very conditions causing despair. By repetition of the quotations already made in a slightly different language, I think we shall discover these conditions. "The whole creation groaneth and travaileth in pain together until now." "Ourselves also groan within ourselves." "The Spirit Himself maketh intercession with groanings which cannot be uttered."

The first of these declarations was the Apostle's recognition of the fact that the whole problem of pain and suffering, of evil in the widest sense, is the problem which constantly confronts the soul of the man of faith in God. It may be well that we remind ourselves that pain presents no problem to any man except to the man who believes in God. Pain becomes a problem only in the presence of faith. Whenever some believer, it may be one whose faith at the moment is trembling, challenges the world's agony, the challenge is always uttered in the presence of the consciousness of God. When the soul cries out in revolt in the presence of the abounding suffering of men, the cry is always born of the wonder how God can permit this. There is no other problem.

Blot God out of His universe, and you will still have pain but no problem to assault the soul. It is only faith that has to face this perplexity. It is Habakkuk who suffers most in the day of the declension of the people of God. It is Habakkuk who says, "Oh, Lord, how long?" I cry murder and You do not hear. I cry violence and there is no answer. What is God doing?

It was Carlyle, rough, rugged, peculiar in many ways and yet a man of the greatest faith, who, when Froude attempted to comfort him by telling him that God is in His heaven, said, "Yes, but He is doing nothing." I never repeat that without being inclined to say to believing souls, Do not be angry with Carlyle. It was not true; God was doing something; but there is neither man nor woman in this house who has ever come very near and remained near to the world's agony, who has not had that thought at some time or another.

The whole creation groaneth and travaileth together in pain, and the proportion of our nearness to God is the proportion of our sense of this problem of pain, for it is the love of God shed abroad in the heart that renders the heart keen and sensitive to the world's agony. The heart of man, taught by the Divine love, questions the Divine love until, presently, the heart of the man discovers that the very agony he feels which makes him question is the result of the presence in his soul of the God of love and, indeed, it is an expression of God's own agony. It is when we become sensible of that prevalent pain that we need hope; and unless hope shall save us, then we shall indeed be lost.

The second state of the apostolic description, "We ourselves groan within ourselves, waiting for our adoption, the redemption of our body," is one of the most illuminating sentences on personal Christian experience in all this writing. The Apostle here describes the increasing sense of failure and shortcomings, the cry and the sob that come out of life with more intense meaning as the years go on: "Wretched man that I am! Who shall deliver me out of the body of this death?" It is the man who comes into the closest association with Christ who also comes to the acutest sense of his own defilement.

We groan within ourselves in the baffling defeat of the soul in its attempt to reach the heights; we wait for the redemption of the body, conscious that the tabernacle in which the spirit dwells is the instrument of defilement for the spirit. It is in hours when the under side of our nature wins its victories that we cry out in agony and almost in despair. It is then that we need the gospel of hope.

Then we come to the last and highest word, most mystic and most difficult of interpretation, "The Spirit Himself maketh intercession for us with groanings that cannot be uttered." In that word we have a description not merely of our sense of the general pain of the world, not merely of our sense of our own particular limitations and defeats but of the Divine discontent which within the soul of a man makes him angry and puts him in agony; that knowledge of God which generates restlessness with everything that is unlike Him and unlike His peace; that hot turbulent protest of the soul against every form of wrong and of tyranny, against the conditions that blight and spoil the universe of God. The Spirit Who knows the deep things of God, the profound emotions of the Divine heart, touches the heart and spirit of a man with the selfsame feelings until the man himself rises unconsciously to a plane of prayer on which he expresses to God the things which God Himself is feeling.

Now, it is this sense of the world's pain, of our own pain, this sense of anger and agony born of our communion with God, that makes hope necessary. These are the things that fill the heart with despair.

What, then, is the hope? This, again, is a most necessary question for consideration, for if it is true that we are saved by hope, it is equally true that men are lost by hope. Unless the hope is true, it destroys. The will-of-the-wisp creates a hope in the heart of the wanderer over the marshes, but it destroys him because it is not a true light. The lights lit by the wreckers along the Cornish shore in the olden days created hope in the heart of many a mariner, but they destroyed. And so, unless hope is true, it will not save, it will destroy.

The Bishop of Durham, Dr. Moule, in his *Commentary on Romans* in the Expositors' Bible, has suggested a trans-

lation of this text which is certainly illuminative. What he
suggests is a fair implication of the text. He suggests that
instead of "We were saved by hope," we render here, "It is
as to our hope that we were saved," as if the text should
mean that we are saved as Christians by hope because of
the nature of the hope that is presented to us.

What, then, is the Christian hope? If we go over these
passages again, we shall find that in every case the hope is
declared. What is our hope for creation? That it shall be
delivered from the bondage of corruption into the liberty of
the children of God. That is one of the greatest sentences in
all the writings of the Apostle. It presents a vision of the
whole creation ultimately led out from the bondage or corruption of that which disintegrates, spoils, mars, ruins into
the liberty of the children of God. A doctrine of the world is
involved in that statement, and it is the biblical doctrine,
the doctrine of the cosmos as under the dominion of man.

The cosmos is seen suffering pain and tribulation because its lord and master, man, has lost his scepter and his
power to govern. That same cosmos will come at last to the
realization of all its beauty and all its glory because the
children of God, men and women after the Divine image
and likeness and fulfilling the Divine relationship, will govern it, so that the creation will realize itself and pass out of
corruption into full and complete realization.

The feeling of the poets helps us here. There lay the
dead sea mew, and Elizabeth Barrett Browning sang,

> Our human touch did on Him pass,
> And with our touch, our agony.

It was the symbol of the whole creation groaning and
travailing together in pain.

Thomas Blake, the father of our Nature poetry, sang:

> A robin redbreast in a cage
> Puts all heaven in a rage;
> A dog starved at his master's gate
> Predicts the ruin of the State.

Superlative language, you say. The superlatives of earth
are the positives of eternity. At last there will be no starved

dog anywhere, no caged robin, no mauled sea mew, nothing left in creation which results from the misgovernment of men. Creation will escape its corruption and enter into the liberty of the glory of the sons of God.

We groan within ourselves, waiting—for what? The adoption, the redemption of the body, the ultimate mastering of the body that it may become the fitting instrument of the spirit. Or as Paul put it when writing to the Philippians of his personal experiences: He "shall fashion a new body of our humiliation, that it may be conformed to the body of His glory."

Concerning that groaning of the spirit, that restlessness of God interpreted to the soul and creating the agony and the power of prayer, what is our hope? The ultimate rest and joy of God in His completed work which, perhaps, we most clearly express when we quote the prophecy and the promise concerning the Messiah Himself, that at last He shall see of the travail of His soul and be satisfied.

The Foundation of This Hope

What are the foundations of this hope? Inclusively, we may say that our hope is set on God, and that through the unveilings of Himself and of His activity which have been granted to us in Christ. To say that is to say everything. God is our hope in the presence of the problem of pain. Our fellowship with Him has created the problem. Who is God? What is God doing? Is God doing anything? Does God care? These are all questions arising out of faith in God.

Blot God out of the heavens, blot God out of the intellectual concept, say there is no God! What then? Ah! but our faith has created our problem, and we shall not solve our problem by denying the God Who created our problem. We have seen a universe in which pain is a wrong, but we should not have seen that if we had not seen God. Therefore, inquiring still more deeply, turning the soul back upon itself, facing the problem, we affirm that the very ultimate ground of hope is God and that the unveiling of Himself which He has given us in Christ is the very inspiration of hope. It is out of that unveiling that hope comes back to us.

Let us inquire a little more particularly about the aspects of these unveilings which inspire hope. And, again, we will confine ourselves to this very passage, for in it the very foundations of hope are laid bare. I base my hope first on the suffering of God, on the fact that the Spirit makes intercession for us with groanings which cannot be uttered; second, on the suffering of the saints, that they who have the first-fruits of the Spirit suffer; and, finally, on the suffering of creation itself. In regard to the creation, the Apostle has linked another word to the word "groaning": "Groaneth and travaileth." It is the word that suggests birth rather than death. This is the wondrous alchemy of Christianity: pain is the ground of confidence that pain will end.

The first ground of hope is that of the suffering of God. "The Spirit maketh intercession for us with groanings that cannot be uttered." "He that searcheth the hearts knoweth what is the mind of the Spirit." "The Spirit searcheth the deep things of God." When we speak here of the Spirit we are thinking of God and included in the thought is that of infinite wisdom, infinite love, infinite power. God, infinite in wisdom, therefore making no mistake; infinite in love, therefore never failing in love, for "Love is not love which alters when it alteration finds"; infinite in power, therefore able to do all that wisdom reveals and love dictates.

The revelation that is given to us of God in our Lord and Savior Jesus Christ is that He is conscious of this agony and is active in the midst of it. He, being the sum total of all things and being more than all the things in which pain is to be found, has gathered the whole within Himself and knows it to its depths. When I look next on the problem of the suffering of the innocent with the guilty, let me remember I am looking on the problem of God's suffering. I admit that this is a problem, a profounder problem than anything London presents or Europe presents or the world presents.

The problem of a suffering God is indeed profound! But there is a solution. It is the solution of a loving God

expressing Himself in a thousand ways in every generation if men had but eyes to see and ears to hear and
hearts to understand; expressing Himself assuredly in
the suffering of every innocent soul that consents to suffering on behalf of the guilty; expressing Himself cen-
trally, and this in some senses finally, in the Cross! You
talk to me of the problem of evil in London. I take you to
the Cross. There it is focused. You talk to me of the
problem of those who suffer. It is centralized in the Cross.
You talk to me of the problem of evil, evil winning, evil
crushing good, evil mauling that which is high and noble. I take you to the Cross. There it is in its vulgar
tragedy, focused, centralized, made vulgar, as it is vulgar!

In that unveiling God has revealed the fact that wherever there is suffering, there is He also. He, the infinitely
wise and loving and powerful, is conscious and active in
the midst of all suffering.

On that I build my palace of hope. I stand in the midst
of the world's agony, and I say this is also the Divine
agony, and therefore my heart believes that at last, how, I
cannot tell, by what methods, I do not know, but at last
the very creation will be delivered from its corruption and
find its way into the glory of the liberty of the children of
that God Who has not absented Himself from human
sorrow, but Who remains within it, gathering its most
poignant power into His own being and vicariously suffering in the midst of the universe blighted by sin.

If I pass from that wider outlook and look again at the
saints, I build my hope on their suffering far more than
on their rejoicing, for in their pain they are sharers of the
Divine pain, making up that which is behind in the suffering of Christ and having fellowship with His suffering.
They are also sharers of the Divine power and of the
Divine patience.

Who are the saints? Take any one Christian man or
woman in the life of this city or far away on the mission
field; take an isolated case for the illumination of the
general fact. What is this man? What is this woman? This
is humanity reborn and regained for God. To use the

word of Jesus, this individual is the seed of the Kingdom. New born souls constitute in earth's soil the seed of the coming Kingdom.

Then I hear the word of the Lord spoken on another occasion, and I link it to this declaration: "Except a grain of wheat fall into the earth and die, it abideth by itself alone." By the suffering of the saints the Kingdom is to come.

This is very well as a general statement. Its particular and personal application must be reserved for loneliness. Let us get away presently, somewhere quite alone, those of us who are suffering in the cause of the Kingdom or in fellowship with the Kingdom or as the result of our loyalty to the Kingdom. Does there seem to be no connection between such suffering and the Kingdom? It is false seeming, for by that suffering, by that pain, by that anguish, we are in fellowship with God; and by that fellowship in pain the victory is to be won, and the Kingdom is to come.

So with the whole creation. I remind you again in a passing sentence only of the suggestiveness of the word, "groaneth and travaileth together in pain." It is the word of birth pangs! The sobbing of creation, its sigh and its agony, are the declaration of its rebirth. "Behold, I make all things new," is the perpetual word of God. He makes all things new by the way of travail. Thus our hope is born of the transmutation of the causes of our despair.

The Effects of This Hope

What are the effects of this hope? I will speak of two only, one named in the immediate context and one named by the Apostle John. The effects are *patience* and *purity*. "We with patience wait." "He that hath his hope set on Him purifieth himself, even as He is pure." What is patience? Patience is simply remaining under. Remaining under in order to bear. To attempt to withdraw is to leave God.

If I am to be in cooperation with God in the processes that are to lead to the final restoration, I must stay in the midst, I must remain under; fellowship with God in service is patience, remaining under, not merely to bear but to lift. To save the life is to lose it, because to withhold the life from pouring out is to exclude God, Who is ever pouring Himself out in sacrifice. The mental experience of such fellowship is patience with God, patience with ourselves, patience with creation.

Patience means staying underneath in fellowship with God because of the assurance, not that at last I shall climb the height, but that at last He will perfect that which concerns me.

The second effect of this hope is that of purity. "Everyone that hath this hope set on Him purifieth himself, even as He is pure." At your leisure, contrast the passage in John with the one in Romans and see how close the thoughts lie to each other. Creation is waiting for the revealing of the sons of God, and we who are the children groan within ourselves waiting for the adoption, the redemption of the body, and the Spirit Himself makes intercession for us with groanings which cannot be uttered. So run the thoughts of Romans. Then I turn to John, and I read, "Beloved, now are we the children of God, but it doth not yet appear what we shall be, for He is not yet manifested." There has been no manifestation yet of this sonship of God in all its finality and its glory and its beauty. But we know that when He shall be manifested as He is, we shall be like Him.

Paul says that creation is waiting for the sons of God. John declares that the Son of God will be manifested with the sons of God. The man who has that hope set on God purifies himself, even as God is pure. The responsibility is that of purification, the type of purity is that of the purity of God.

If that were all, I hardly dare read the passage. Is there power for such purification? The Apostle goes on to declare that He was manifested to destroy the works of the devil.

And so as we are conscious of the sorrows of the world, the perils threatening us in our home life, the perils of our prosperity, the persistence of pain everywhere, the failure and disappointment verging on despair, we are saved by hope! Our hope is built on Him Who is our God. Our hope, therefore, is based also on the very sense of defeat and despair and pain that cause our agony; for by these things men live, by these defeats they climb to the higher heights, by these bruisings and these batterings of the iron, life is molded and shaped to the Divine purpose. The only man who has no hope is the man who has no God.

But that must not be the last note. The last note must be this: God is our abiding hope, and by hope we are saved.

Hope and Patience

John Ker (1819–1886) is little known today, but in his day he was a respected preacher and professor of preaching and pastoral work at the United Free Church Seminary in Glasgow, Scotland. He published two volumes of sermons.

This one is from the *Sermons First Series*, published in Edinburgh in 1870 by Edmonston and Douglas.

John Ker

9

HOPE AND PATIENCE

It is good that a man should both hope and quietly wait for the salvation of the Lord (Lamentations 3:26).

THERE ARE few parts of the Bible where in so short a compass as this chapter there is shown such a bitterness of sorrow and such a strength of consolation. The grief and comfort pursue each other like the shadows and sunshine of a day in spring. A mighty wave breaks over the man's head and all seems lost, but we see him again standing on firm ground, and his voice comes out not in cries for help but in expressions of confidence. He is afflicted in body and depressed in soul, assailed by enemies and grieved by the state of God's cause, but one thing constantly reappears to sustain him—the view of God Himself. And if the sky overhead will clear in this way though at intervals, we can hold on when all the earth is wrapped in gloom. It is from heaven and not from earth that a believing man expects the outcome of the sun. You find, therefore, that his eye looks upward; and, when it cannot see God, it seeks the place where He is hidden, as a flower bends its head toward the cloud which veils the light.

God and His salvation are the object of his desire. Gladly would he possess them, but if he cannot, he will make them the object of his hope; and if hope fails, he will quietly wait. There is no case so desperate—no weary disappointment so prolonged—in which there does not remain some duty toward God. This is what we have to consider. In the 24th verse this sufferer speaks of his hope in God: "The Lord is my portion, saith my soul, therefore will I *hope* in Him." In the 25th verse he speaks of "waiting for God": "The Lord is good unto them that *wait* for Him, to the soul that seeketh Him." And here in the 26th verse, he combines the two: "It is good that a man should both *hope* and quietly *wait* for the salvation of the Lord."

We shall, *first*, consider what is meant by the "salvation of the Lord"; *next*, the separate exercises of the soul toward it; and, *lastly*, the benefit of conjoining these— "both to hope and quietly to wait."

The Meaning of "Salvation"

The FIRST thing is to understand what is meant by the *"salvation of the Lord."*

Now, God's salvation is used very frequently in the Bible for His interposition to save the soul of man from sin—that great salvation which is the sum and substance of the Bible. A man becomes possessed of it when in humble trust he commits his soul to God's mercy, as it is made known. We do not think, however, that it is this salvation which is here spoken of for though a man may be encouraged "to hope," he cannot be urged "quietly to wait for it." He is to strive—to ask and seek and knock until he finds; but there is not a spot in the search after God where he is entitled to sit down and rest. If we look, moreover, into the language of the chapter, we shall see that it is not that of a man who is ignorant of God. He is acquainted with His gracious character and has learned to rely on it.

The "salvation of the Lord" here is something else than the first view which a sinful man obtains of pardon and peace through "the great God our Savior." It is the salvation which a man needs in any crisis of life, where he suffers under trial or is threatened with it. And in these trials, hope and quiet waiting do not come at once into their fullest exercise. As long as human means can avail, it is a man's duty, trusting to Divine help, to employ them. To sit and wait where effort can avail is to insult God's providence. The "salvation of the Lord" is when all conceivable means have been employed and have failed. The hand can do, the heart can devise nothing more. When the Israelites had reached the Red Sea with the mountains on either side and the Egyptians behind, the words of Moses were, "Stand still, and see *the salvation of God.*"

Such positions are frequently arrived at in life. We feel that we are at the end of all endeavor, and the object has not been gained. Our strength and resources—all possible expedients—have been brought into exercise. The last reserve has been thrown into the battle, and yet it goes against us. We may struggle on with a blind despair, and as long as strength remains, we must struggle on; but this power too seems to be failing. It is then that the case rises distinctly into *"the salvation of the Lord."* Nothing can save us but His marked interposition, and the heart must put itself in the attitude of "hope and quiet waiting" for it.

The trials of this kind are innumerable, as varied as the lives of men, and when we instance one or two, we know that we touch only the surface of human experience.

There may be some who are using every endeavor to secure subsistence and an honorable position for themselves and those dependent on them; and yet all their efforts are unsuccessful. Slowly the tide of comfort and even of the means of existence is ebbing; and the dark reefs which threaten utter shipwreck lift their head. If some change does not quickly come, they feel that temporal ruin is on them. It is a time not to relax effort but to look out more intently for deliverance from God and to have the heart resting on it.

Or there may be someone who has the presence of a constant difficulty in the spiritual life—perhaps the want of that sense of religious comfort which is felt to be so desirable or the obtrusion of some painful doubt about doctrine or duty through which no present light can be seen. To cast the thing aside and become indifferent to it would be against the promptings of the whole spiritual nature; and yet to reconcile it with other convictions is meanwhile impossible. There are many such cases of painful want of harmony in our time. A period occurs in every genuine life when the simple faith of childhood has to pass over into the intelligent faith of manhood, and such periods occur also in the history of the world. Many things then seem shaken when they are only about to be established on new and higher ground.

If there are some who are involved in such a struggle and if all thought has failed to open a path through it, it is a time also for this more entire reliance upon God. No exertion to reach light is to be neglected, but there may be a more implicit confidence in Him who is the Father of lights—holding steadfastly to what is felt to be true and waiting for illumination on what is doubtful—"casting out the anchor and wishing for the day."

Perhaps there are some who are deeply interested in the spiritual welfare of a soul dear to them as their own. Their prayer has been rising like that of Abraham for Ishmael, "O that he might live before God!" But all means have appeared to fail. If there is not positive disregard of religion, there is at least want of that thorough decision which is so longed for by those who know the full value of God's friendship and who yearn to see all that their heart loves most included in it. There is a certain length we can go in such endeavors, and we feel that to go further might injure the end we seek. Then this remains to us—to take all our endeavor and leave it with God in whose hand are the hearts of all men, who can follow the wanderer wherever his feet or his thoughts may carry him and can bring him again to Himself and to His Father's house.

Or it may be, there is some life which has lost all the relish it once possessed—where wasting sickness has undermined the strength—or friends who were the hue and perfume of it have been taken away—or hopes that hung on its horizon like a coming glory have melted into thin air—and existence seems to have no more an object, and duty sinks into a dull mechanical round, and the night comes down dark and starless, and the morning rises cold and colorless. It is hard to say what can restore to such a life its vigor and freshness, for the mind comes oftentimes to have a morbid love of the gloom which is its misery and to reckon it treason to its past hopes to turn its eye from their sepulcher. God only knows the remedy, and it is a special time to call up higher duty to our aid—the duty of turning to Him and striving to feel that He has it in His power, though we may not see how, to save us over the grave of our most cherished hopes without causing us to forget them and to shine in with a reviving light upon the dullest and bleakest of earthly walks.

There is, probably, not one of us but has some such trial as these—some object on which our heart has been set, not yet attained or taken away from us beyond the prospect of recovery. We stand at the end of all our exertion, and our desire is far out of our reach. A man who has faith only in worldly resources is powerless here. He must give up in despair or cast himself on a blind chance. But for a believing man, there is still a duty and a stay. When he cannot take a step further in human effort, there is a pathway to the sky, and his heart can travel it.

There is a "salvation of the Lord" which lies beyond and above every deliverance in the power or even the conception of man: "Hast thou not known, hast thou not heard, that the everlasting God, the Lord, the Creator of the ends of the earth, fainteth not, neither is weary? There is no searching of His understanding." Then comes the time to realize this—that if the object of our desire is right and good, He can give it to us in a way we dream not of and that, if it is denied, it is because there is something better in store, "above what we ask or think." Some hidden treasure of the soul is to be opened up, or some future gain of the immortal life is being prepared by this delay.

The blessing we long for can come in this world, sudden and wonderful, written all over with the manifest tokens of God's hand; or if it may never be ours here, it carries the standard of hope beyond the gulf to plant it on the shores of the eternal. We may quietly wait with the assurance that every blessing will be found complete when those who trust in Him are saved in the Lord with an everlasting salvation.

The Means of Salvation

The SECOND thing is to consider what is meant by these exercises of the soul toward God's salvation—"*to hope, and quietly to wait.*"

Every one of us knows without any labored definition

what it is to *hope*. But if we are to set ourselves to practice it in a Christian way, it may be useful to look at some
of its elements.

The foundation of hope may be said to lie in *desire*. It
differs from desire in this, that desire pursues many things
that can never be objects of hope to us. We can only hope
for that which is felt to be possible and reasonable. This
then is the first thing for us to do if we would strengthen
hope, to see that its objects are right and good—that is,
accordant with the Divine will and beneficial for us. We
may learn this by consulting God's Word and our own
thoughtful experience. We are sure never to err when we
begin with the blessings that concern our spiritual and
immortal nature.

We may wish without fear and without limit for whatever brings us nearer to God's friendship and fellowship—
for whatever forms in us the mind and likeness of Christ.
After this we are perfectly free to desire those things
which meet the wants of our entire nature, as far as these
are sinless. That nature is of God's making, and all its
necessities and affections have true and proper objects.
But on this human side, we should never wish with the
same absolute strength, for we live in a world where the
lower comes often into conflict with the higher; and we
should seek to desire things in their due proportion—
first, the kingdom of God and His righteousness and then
all the other things that may be fitly added to it. If we
have been taught thus to govern our desires, we have laid
the foundation of well-grounded hope.

The next element in Christian hope is *faith*. Hope differs
from faith in this, that we believe in many things in regard
to which we do not hope. Hope is faith with desire pointing
out the objects. If we have sought to make these desires
Christian and reasonable, then we may consistently call in
the aid of faith. "The Lord shall give that which is good."
We have the assurance in the knowledge of Him as the
"Father of spirits," that He will care for the souls He has
made. If we give up to His keeping that precious and immortal part of our nature, we may have the most perfect
conviction that He will satisfy all the longings He has in-

fused into it and will fill it with all the happiness of which it is capable. And as He is the "God of the spirits of all flesh"—of spirits which dwell in fleshly tabernacles and which are open, therefore, to joys and sorrows dependent on them—we may be sure that He will not overlook this part of our nature. Only His care of it will be proportioned to that same importance which we have been taught to observe in our desires.

So we may reason from the general spirit of the Bible; when we go to its particular promises, we find them every one bearing out this view. They tell us that the spiritual, as it is to be unfolded and perfected in the eternal, is the great concernment of God's dealings with us; but that in subordination to this, all that belongs to our happiness is the object of His care and may be the subject of our hope. The greater end does not finally exclude the less; it only modifies and regulates it and makes it in its last issue more certain and complete. The hope of the Bible is first of all divine, like its great subject, but it is also like Him, truly and tenderly human. For a time they are in outward conflict, the human crying out in suffering and struggle but all the while sustained by the divine and destined at last to enter into a visible and glorious harmony with it.

When we have sought to purify our desires and to make them the subject of faith as far as they are right and good, there is still a third element to be added to make our hope strong—that of *imagination*. I know that this word is misjudged by many and associated, if not with the sinful, at least with the visionary. But it is a true, God-given part of human nature and ready to be turned to the noblest use. While sin has made it a charnel-house of corruption or a storehouse of vanities, purity can fill its treasury with divine aspirations which are as grand as they are transcendently real. It is that power of the soul which gives to hope its wings. Let it but rise from the desire of what is true and good and be chastened by the faith of what God has promised, and it can lift up the soul above the most terrible trials and put it already in possession of the unseen and heavenly.

No one can read the Bible without seeing that it has

everywhere its Pisgahs and Tabors and exceeding high mountains, whence the beauty and glory of the future are to be discerned—and God's Spirit carries men to their summit and bids them open their eyes. It is true that all cannot rise to the same height nor look with the same vision, but in every nature the faculty of the ideal lies hidden, and religion was intended above all things else to call it forth. Every true Christian has the soul of the poet latent in his nature. If many are kept depressed and earth-attracted, it is because they do not strive enough to free this power from sinful and worldly encumbrances and to give it wings to soar to its native home.

Let us dwell more on those scenes of the invisible and future which are depicted in God's Word and of which the renewed heart has the presentiment in itself, and while the imagination gives vividness to these pictures, faith will give reality to them. For it tells us that in the degree in which they are good for us, they must be ours. Even in regard to the deliverances and blessings which we may desire from God in our present life, we are not required to forecast the issue in colorless vagueness. As we may wish and pray for definite things, so we may imagine them and try to think how God may and can bestow them.

The imagination which is permitted to others is not forbidden to a Christian—only with him it will not be so positive as to dictate God's way of realizing it. He will seek to feel in all his forecastings that God can do to him above what he can think and that even in this world it does not enter into man's heart to conceive what God prepares for them that love Him. What he hopes for, whether of the heavenly or earthly, will still be the *salvation of the Lord*.

The next exercise of soul which we are to cherish toward God's interpositions is *"quiet waiting."*

There come times in life when as labor seems vain and resultless, so also hope droops and is ready to die. The strong emotions of our nature do not continue long with equal freshness. The laws of action and reaction, as in material things, come into operation, and in proportion to excitement which has strained nature, there is depression. It would save some Christians much grief and vain self-reproach if they would remember this. We are often no more accountable for our moods than for our temperament. After seasons of excessive emotion, there will come times of lassitude sinking to torpor. Both have their *use*. The shadow is as necessary for growth as the sunshine, and these alternations give the Christian graces their full proportion in the character. Both have their *duties*. Though we may not be responsible for moods, we are for the way in which we act under them. When all our endeavor fails, we are to fall back on hope, and when hope begins to faint, there is still left to us "quiet waiting." So full of resources is the grace of God, that as each lower deep of trouble opens, a new power in the Christian life can be created to meet it.

"Quiet waiting" is that which in other parts of the Bible and especially in the New Testament is termed patience. It is the part of hope to seek the future; it is the duty of patience to rest calmly in the present and not to fret—to be satisfied to be where God appoints and to suffer what God sends. It is fitly placed after hope, because it follows it in the natural course of an educated Christian life.

Hope belongs to youth; patience is the lesson of maturity. Hope enters with a man into his first battle, perhaps in some forms it is never brighter than then—the helmet-hope of salvation has been dimmed and dented by no blow; but patience is the hard acquirement of the veteran, gained in many a march and campaign. So it was unfolded for our example in the Captain of our salvation who endured God's will after He had done it and took the cup of trial patiently into His hand when He had finished His active work.

As there are means for stimulating hope, so there are also for strengthening patience, and there is in some measure a correspondence in them.

One means is common to both—the employment of *faith*. It will enable us more quietly to wait if we have confidence in the all-wise and all-merciful arrangements of God. The failures—the seeming blanks and dull monotonies of life—which try our patience most are equally at

His disposal with its highest activities and enjoyments, and the very wildernesses and solitary places of it may be those which shall yet rejoice and blossom like the rose. He can make all its wastes to be as Eden and bring out the best spiritual results from what seem to us the most barren spots.

In other respects, the means for growing in patience are very different from those that help hope. If hope is nursed by desire of what we have not, patience is maintained by *contentment with what we have*. Our duty may be, when desire of something lost or longed for is consuming us, to bend our look more intently on the present and try to discover how many things, and how precious, God has left to us. There are situations in life which to the outside spectator appear the most dark and cheerless that are far from being so to those who are in the center of them. Bright spots come out and sources of interest open up which common eyes disregard; and we learn that life may be like the homes of some Eastern lands which have their dull, dead walls to the crowd, but their fountains and flowers and singing birds in the courts within.

There are many joys with which a stranger cannot intermeddle, which he cannot even discern, and if we are to wait quietly, we must cultivate an eye for these. One purpose of our detention may be that we may discover them, for both in the natural and Christian life, men lose what is near in their haste to reach the distant. Nay, more, if they reached the future it would disappoint them, for it is only to those who have learned to draw from the present its hidden stores that the future can yield its true and rich treasures. It is not necessary that we should shut out hope as one of these sources of present interest, but we must admit it as the handmaid of patience, not as its mistress, and we must treat it so that we can feel thankful there are many other things besides hope which still abide.

Then instead of that imagination which nourishes hope, we must cultivate patience by a calm attention to duties. Quiet waiting is not inaction. We may be waiting for one object while we are steadily working for another. If some aim which engrossed our life is withdrawn and some way of usefulness which had all our affection is closed, we shall find there are other roads to walk in and other works to perform, provided the heart will accept them. Even though the heart shrinks, if the hand will only give itself to what it finds to do and will do it with its might, the heart will follow.

It is a kind law of our nature that labor expended on any object gives an interest in it; it is a still kinder law of the kingdom of God that the tamest and most insignificant of daily duties may be made noble and divine when the thought of God and the will of Christ are carried into them. One soul may rise to heroism in the narrowest circle of routine when another dwindles upon the grandest fields of action.

Thus the means are at our disposal for building up these virtues of hope and patience in our character. When we give our souls up in trust to God, He gives them back to us again with His hand on them, that we may labor to fill them with all that can make them happy in the future and strong in the present.

The Union of Hope and Patience

We come now, in the THIRD place, to consider the benefit of uniting these—"It is good *both* to hope and quietly to wait."

But is it possible to unite them? It would seem as if hope and patience were at open war. Hope carries us to the future; patience binds us to the present. Hope has a restless fire and energy; the strength of patience is in calm and often in unresisting endurance. We can see as we look around how ready men are to run into one or other of the extremes—how some natures are over-sanguine and unsteadfast, others submissive to all that comes with a dull despondency. Yet it is for this very reason that the two are conjoined and that we are urged to aim at the true balance. If we feel that our nature tends to either side, we must strive with God's help to correct it by its opposite.

We know how in material laws forces which counteract each other can combine in harmony. The attraction that holds our world to the sun is met by the impulse which propels it straight into space, and the movement which gives us day and night, summer and winter, is the result of both. Every Christian heart feels how it can be going forward in thought to some blessing God has promised and yet resting while it is withheld in submission to the Divine will—as John, in Patmos, walked the streets of the heavenly city and listened to its songs and yet abode in his solitary exile and was satisfied to be there as long as God required.

That we may be led to aim at both of these, consider this, that *the one is needful to save the other from sinking into sin.* If hope possessed the Christian heart alone, it would be ready to flutter itself into impatience. The brighter the future rose upon the vision, the more the man would fret against the delay. Hope left to itself would be an ill-disciplined child that cries for what its heart is set upon and will hear of no denial. It would soon cease to be hope—its clear eye would be dim with tears of discontent, and its heart would sink for the distance from its goal.

On the other hand, if we had quiet waiting without hope, it would be in danger of settling into stagnancy. The object of its waiting would disappear, and trials without any end in view would benumb and paralyze it. Hope without patience would be life kindling into over-intensity and burning itself out in fruitless longings. Patience without hope would be the decay of life's flame for want of nourishment, till it would sink into the quietude of death.

Whenever hope rises into impatience, it is the will of God that quiet waiting should lay its hand upon it and bid it "rest in the Lord and wait patiently for Him and not fret," for there is purpose in His delay and occupation meanwhile for us. When patient waiting on its side becomes indifferent or torpid, it is not less the will of God that hope should come and wake it up, as the cry did the slumbering virgins, "Behold, the bridegroom cometh, go ye forth to meet Him." On either side we may fall into sin, and the fully approved state is to have the eye looking forward while the heart is at rest—to combine these two as they are found so often combined in the Bible by the

Psalmist (130:5), "I wait for the Lord, my soul doth wait, and in his word do I hope"—by the Apostle (1 Thess. 1:3), "the patience of hope in our Lord Jesus Christ"—and by the speaker here, "both to hope and quietly to wait for the salvation of the Lord."

Consider this also, that *the one is needful to raise the other to its full strength.* Christian patience rises to its proper power not through any force of insensibility. It is thoughtful and reasonable and must know where it is and what it waits for. It is the part of hope to tell it this— to throw into it the light of intelligence and make it strong with the promises and the power of God. The Savior still leaves us, as He left His first disciples in the garden with the words, "Tarry ye here and watch," and promises to come again. If hope can lay hold of this promise and keep it fast, patience will maintain its post like a sentinel who is sure of relief at the appointed hour. If the hour seems long, it will beguile it with those words which have passed like a "song in the night" through many a weary heart— "For yet a little while, and He that shall come will come, and will not tarry."

Then as hope strengthens patience, patience in return will strengthen hope. Such allies are all the Christian graces. Children in one family who, if there is love among them, supplement each other by their opposites. If a man is enabled to "rest in the Lord, and wait patiently for Him," it is a reason to him for hoping that there is a divine work going on in his life which the God of patience and consolation will complete.

If I can feel that there is a strength which bears me up under heavy burdens and lonely hours, I can trust it for more than this. I must trust it for more, since my inmost heart feels that patience is only the means of my life's walk and not its end, and God does not intend to deceive us either by our human or our Christian instincts. Patience brooding over its own quiet spirit, which yet it feels is not its own, has the presentiment and augury of an end beyond itself. In the deep well of a tranquil heart, the star of hope is lying—ever clearer as the calm is deepening— reflected down into it from God's own heaven.

This is God's manner, first, to give the inward peace of soul and afterward the final deliverance. He came into the ship and calmed the disciples' fears, and then He spoke and calmed the storm: "I will be with thee in trouble"; and then it follows, "I will deliver thee." Peter's prison was opened by the prayers of friends without, but that of Paul and Silas was burst by the song within, and this is something nobler and better.

When God gives to us this patience which can rise even to triumph, we may begin to rejoice in hope and be sure that He will proclaim liberty to the captives. It is the order of that golden chain (Rom. 5:3), "Knowing that tribulation worketh patience; and patience, experience; and experience, hope: and hope maketh not ashamed; because the love of God is shed abroad in our hearts by the Holy Spirit, which is given unto us."

And now if it be possible to unite these two and if it be so needful, it should be the lesson of our life daily to aim at it—to hope without impatience and to wait without despondency—to fold the wing in captivity like a caged bird and be ready to use the pinion when He breaks our prison. Let us address ourselves with a cheerful endurance to our duties, whether they weary us by their weight or by their trivial monotony—and to trials, whether they come in great afflictions or in fretting and ever-recurring vexations. We may attain to that hopeful patience which comes not from stoicism but Christianity, which feels all the good of life and yet can be strong and satisfied in the want of it—the finest acquirement of that higher school which the gospel has introduced, "I have learned, in whatsoever state I am, therewith to be content."

We shall find increasingly "how good it is." It is good now *in the depth of the soul*—in the conscious assurance that it is better to rest in the hardest of God's ways than to wander at will in our own. "Behold, we count them happy who endure." We shall find it good in the growth of all the Christian graces under the shadow of patience. Were we to gain every blessing so soon as sought, the blessing itself would be small, and we should gain nothing more. But now while we patiently wait, faith becomes stronger, resignation sinks into a deeper attitude of reverence, gentleness and meekness are clothed with softer beauty, and courage and fortitude and all the stronger powers of the soul arouse themselves and put on armor "to endure hardness as good soldiers of Jesus Christ."

We shall find how good it is *in the enhancement of every blessing for which we have to wait.* God's plan of providing blessings for us is to educate the capacity which is to receive them. We are straitened in ourselves and must be kept waiting till our minds and hearts enlarge. "Ye have need of patience, that, after ye have done the will of God, ye might receive the promise." Between your use of all the means and the result which you desire, there is still a gulf of separation on the brink of which patience must sit and look across, waiting God's time and way to pass it. And when patience has her perfect work, "ye shall be perfect and entire, wanting nothing" (James 1:4). Then the result will come—the full blessing you desire or something better.

And at the close of all, the pilgrims are kept resting on the river's bank in view of the celestial city till the Lord send His message for them to cross the stream. If they have a right heart, it will be growing larger while they wait, and the provisions of the born will enlarge to meet it. For while they are waiting, Christ is working to prepare the place. "Be patient, therefore, brethren, unto the coming of the Lord."

Of all the motives to hopeful endurance, surely this last is not the smallest, that He who lays the duty upon us has Himself given the example of it. He asks nothing from us that He has not done for us and done by a harder road and with a heavier burden. If there are some of us who have not begun to think of the "salvation of the Lord" in any way, let us turn the eye to Him who did so much to bring it within our view and reach.

The only recompense we can make Him is to seek to be part of his joy and crown. And if we have been the course which with all its struggles is a happy and a hopeful one, let us keep the eye fixed on Him who is our Surety, our Forerunner, and our Prize, and "let us run with patience the race that is set before us, looking unto Jesus, the author and finisher of our faith; who, for the joy that was set before Him, endured the cross, despising the shame, and is set down at the right hand of the throne of God."

NOTES

The Hope Laid Up in Heaven

Charles Haddon Spurgeon (1834–1892) is undoubtedly the most famous minister of the last century. Converted in 1850, he united with the Baptists and soon began to preach in various places. He became pastor of the Baptist church in Waterbeach in 1851, and three years later he was called to the decaying Park Street Church, London. Within a short time, the work began to prosper, a new church was built and dedicated in 1861, and Spurgeon became London's most popular preacher. In 1855, he began to publish his sermons weekly; and today they make up the fifty-seven volumes of *The Metropolitan Tabernacle Pulpit*. He founded a pastor's college and several orphanages.

This sermon is taken from *The Metropolitan Tabernacle Pulpit*, volume 24. He preached it on Sunday morning, October 13, 1878.

Charles Haddon Spurgeon

10

THE HOPE LAID UP IN HEAVEN

For the hope which is laid up for you in heaven, whereof ye heard before in the word of the truth of the gospel (Colossians 1:5).

THREE GRACES should be always conspicuous in Christians—faith, love, and hope. They are each mentioned by Paul in the opening verses of the epistle from which our text is taken. These lovely graces should be so conspicuous in every believer as to be spoken of and consequently heard of even by those who have never seen us. These flowers should yield so sweet a perfume that their fragrance may be perceived by those who have never gazed upon them. So was it with the saints at Colosse. Paul says, "We give thanks to God and the Father of our Lord Jesus Christ, praying always for you, since we *heard* of your *faith* in Christ Jesus, and of the *love* which ye have to all the saints, for the *hope* which is laid up for you in heaven."

May our characters be such as can be reported of without causing us to blush, but that can never be the case if these essential virtues are absent. If these things are in us and abound, we shall not be barren or unfruitful, but if they are lacking, we are as withered branches. We should therefore be rich in faith which is the root of every grace; to this end we should daily pray, "Lord, increase our faith." We should strive to be full even to overflowing with love which is of God and makes us like to God; we should also abound in hope, even that heavenly hope which causes a man to purify himself in readiness for the inheritance above. See to it that neither of these three divine sisters are strangers to your souls, but let faith, hope, and love take up their abode in your hearts.

Note, however, the special character of each of these graces as it exists in the Christian. It is not every faith and love and hope that will serve our turn, for of all precious things there are counterfeits. There is a kind of *faith* in all men, but ours is *faith in Christ Jesus*, faith in Him whom the world rejects, whose cross is a stumbling block and whose doctrine is an offense. We have faith in the man of Nazareth who is also the Son of God, faith in Him who having made atonement by His own blood once for all is now exalted to His Father's right hand. Our confidence is not placed in ourselves nor in any human priest nor in the traditions of our fathers nor in the teachings of human wisdom but alone in Christ Jesus. This is the faith of God's elect.

The *love* of Christians too is also special. For while a Christian is moved by universal benevolence and desires to do good unto all men, yet he has a special love *unto all the saints*, and these the world loves not because it loves not their Lord. The true believer loves the persecuted, the misrepresented, and despised people of God for Christ's sake. He loves them all even though he may think some of them to be mistaken in minor matters. He has love to the babes in grace as well as to the grown saints and love even to those saints whose infirmities are more manifest than their virtues. He loves them not for their station or for their natural amiability but because Jesus loves them and because they love Jesus. You see the faith is in Christ Jesus, but the love extends beyond Christ Himself to all those who are in union with Him, while hope takes a still wider sweep and includes the eternal future in its circuit, thus do our graces increase in range as well as in number.

Our *hope* too upon which we are to speak this morning is special, because it is a hope which is laid up for us in heaven, a hope therefore which the worldling cares not one whit about. He hopes that tomorrow may be as this day and yet more abundant, but he cares nothing for the land where time has ceased to flow. He hopes for riches or he hopes for fame; he hopes for long life and prosperity; he hopes for pleasure and domestic peace; the whole range of his hope is within the compass of his eye. But our hope has passed beyond the sphere of sight, according to the word of the apostle, "What a man seeth, why doth he yet hope for? But if we hope for that we see not, then do we with patience wait for it." Ours is a hope which demands nothing of time or earth but seeks its all in the world to come. It is of this hope that we are about to speak. May the Holy Spirit lead us into a profitable meditation upon it.

The connection of our text seems to be this: the apostle so much rejoiced when he saw the saints at Colosse possessing faith, love, and hope that he thanked God and prayed about them. He saw these seals of God upon them, these three tokens that they were a really converted people, and his heart was glad. All the faithful ministers of Christ rejoice to see their people adorned with the jewels of faith and love and hope, for these are their ornament for the present and their preparation for the future. This I believe to be the connection, but yet from the form of the language, it is clear that the apostle intended to state that their love to the saints was very much produced in them by the hope which was laid up in heaven.

You notice the word "for," which stands there: "The love which ye have to all the saints for," or *on account of* or *because of*, "the hope which is laid up for you in heaven." There can be no doubt that the hope of heaven tends greatly to foster love to all the saints of God. We have a common hope, let us have a common affection; we are on our way to God, let us march in loving company; we are to be one in heaven, let us be one on earth. One is our Master and one is our service; one is our way and one is our end; let us be knit together as one man. We all of us expect to see our Well-beloved face to face and to be like Him; why should we not even now love all those in whom there is anything of Christ?

Beloved, we are to live together forever in heaven. It is a pity we should quarrel. We are forever to be with Jesus Christ, partakers of the same joy, of the same glory, and of the same love; why should we be scant in our love to each other? On the way to Canaan we have to fight the same enemy, to publish the same testimony, to bear the same trials, and to fly to the same helper; therefore let us love one another. It were not difficult to show that the hope which is laid up in heaven should be productive of love among the saints on earth.

This connection of my text with the clause immediately before it does not at all prevent its being regarded in the sense which I first mentioned, namely, that it was a subject for joy with the apostle that the Colossians had faith and love and hope, for he would rejoice nonetheless because their faith was fostered by their hope. It commends these sweet graces that they are so wonderfully inter-twisted with each other and dependent upon one another. There would be no love to the saints if there were not faith in Christ Jesus, and if there were not faith in Christ Jesus, there would be no hope laid up in heaven. If we had no love, it would be certain that we had no truth, and if we had no hope, faith would be assuredly absent. If we entertain one of the graces, we must receive her sisters, for they cannot be separated. Here are three brilliants set in the same golden setting, and none must break the precious jewel. "Now abideth faith, hope, and love, these three," and blessed is he who has them abiding in his own heart.

Now we will let faith and love stand by for a little while, and we will talk about hope, the hope mentioned in our text, the hope which is laid up for you in heaven. First, *it is a very marvelous hope*; secondly, *it is a very secure hope*; and thirdly, *it is a very powerfully influential hope*. May the Holy Ghost bless these thoughts to us all.

A Marvelous Hope

First, then, we speak of our hope which is laid up for us in heaven as a VERY MARVELOUS HOPE, and it is so if we only consider that *it is a great act of grace that sinners should have a hope at all*. That when man had broken his Maker's law there should remain a hope for him is a thought which should make our hearts leap with gratitude. Do you not recollect when you felt it to be so? When sin lay heavily upon your conscience, Satan came and wrote over the lintel of your door, "No HOPE," and the grim sentence would have stood there to this day had not a loving hand taken the hyssop and by a sprinkling of precious blood removed the black inscription. "Wherefore remember that at that time ye were without Christ, having no hope, and without God in the world."

That was our condition once; it is a marvelous thing that it should be thoroughly changed and that assurance should have taken the place of despair. In our carnal estate many false hopes like will-o'-the-wisps danced before us, deceived us, and led us into bogs of presumption and error, but we really had no hope. This is a dreadful condition for a man to be in. It is indeed the very worst of all; never is the storm so terrible as when in the howling of the winds the man distinctly hears the words "*No hope.*" Yet into the thick darkness of NO HOPE we once steered our course, and each time we tried to rely upon good works, outward ceremonies, and good resolutions, we were disappointed anew, and the words rung into our souls with dread monotony, "No hope, no hope," until we wanted to lie down and die. Now sinners though we be, we have a hope. Ever since by faith we looked to Jesus on the cross, a hope full of glory has taken possession of our hearts. Is this not a marvelous thing?

More marvelous still is it *that our hope should venture to be associated with heaven.* Can there be heaven for such as we are? It seems almost presumptuous for a sinner who so richly deserves hell even to lift up his eyes toward heaven. He might have some hope of purgatory, if there were such a region, but a hope of heaven, is not that too much? Yet, beloved, we have no fear of hell or of purgatory now, but we expect to taste the joys laid up in heaven. There is no purgatory for anyone, and there is no hell for saints; heaven awaits all believers in Jesus. Our hope is full of glory, for it has to do with the glory of Christ whom we hope to behold.

Do you expect then, you who were black with lust, that you shall sit among the angels? "Ay, that I do," saith the believer, "and nearer to the throne than they." And you who have plunged into every form of uncleanness, do you expect to see God, for none but the pure in heart can behold Him? "Aye, that I do," saith he, "and not only to see Him, but to be like His Son, when I see Him as He is."

What a divine hope is this! Not that we shall sit down on heaven's doorstep and hear stray notes of the songs within, but that we shall sing with the happy band; not that we shall have an occasional glance within the gates of pearl and feel our hearts hankering after the unutterable joys within the sacred enclosure, but we shall actually and personally enter into the halls of the palace and see the King in His beauty in the land which is very far off.

This is a brave hope, is it not? Why, she aspires to all that the best of saints have received. She looks for the same vision of glory, the same ecstasy of delight. She even aspires to sit upon the throne of Christ, according to the promise, "To him that overcometh will I grant to sit with me in my throne, even as I also overcame, and am set down with my Father in his throne." Hope reckons to be among the overcomers and to partake in their enthronement. This is marvelous hope for a struggling believer to entertain, yet it is not presumption, but confidence warranted by the Word of God. Is it not a miracle of love that such poor creatures as ourselves should be enabled thus to hope in God?

This hope is the more marvelous because *it is so substantial.* In our text the apostle scarcely seems to be speaking of the grace of hope, since that can hardly be said to be laid up in heaven but dwells in our bosoms. He rather speaks of the *object* of hope, and yet it is clear that in his mind the grace of hope as well as the object must have been intended, because that which is laid up in heaven is not a hope except to those who hope for it; it is clear that no man has a hope laid up in heaven unless he has hope within himself.

The truth is that the two things—the grace of hope and its object—are here mentioned under one term which may be intended to teach us that when hope is wrought in the heart by the Holy Spirit, it is the thing hoped for, even as faith is the thing believed, because it realizes and secures it. Just as faith is the substance of things hoped for and the evidence of things not seen, so is hope the substance of the thing it expects and the evidence of the thing it cannot see.

Paul in this case, as in many others, uses language rather according to the theological sense which he would convey than according to the classical usage of the Greek tongue. The words of a heathen people must be somewhat strained from their former use if they are to express divine truth, and Paul does thus stretch them to their utmost length in this case. The hope of the true believer is so substantial that Paul even speaks of it as though it were the thing itself and were laid up in heaven. Many a man has a hope of wealth, but that hope is a different thing from being wealthy. There is many a slip 'twixt the cup and the lip, saith the old proverb, and how true it is!

A man may have a hope of old age, yet he may never reach even middle life, and thus it is clear that the hope of long life is not in itself longevity. But he that hath the divine hope which grows out of faith and love hath a hope which shall never be disappointed, so that the apostle speaks of it as being identical with the thing hoped for and describes it as laid up in heaven. What a marvelous hope is this which long before its realization is treated as a matter of actual attainment and spoken of as a treasure reserved in the coffers of heaven!

One marvelous point about our hope is this, that it is the subject of divine revelation. No one could ever have invented this hope; it is so glorious as to baffle imagination. The prince of dreamers could never have dreamed it, nor the master of the art of logic have inferred it by reason. Imagination and understanding are both left upon the ground while the Bible idea of heaven soars upward like a strong-winged angel. The eternal hope had to be revealed to us; we should never have known it else, for the apostle says, "Whereof ye heard before in the word of the truth of the gospel."

That a sinful man should have a hope of enjoying the perfect bliss of Paradise is a thing not to be thought of were it not that the Lord has promised it. I say again, imagination's utmost stretch had never reached to this, neither could we have had the presumption to suppose that such a bliss could be in store for men so unworthy and undeserving, had we not been assured thereof by the

Word of God. But now the Word of God has opened a window in heaven and bidden us look therein and hope for the time when we shall drink of its living fountains of waters and go no more out forever.

This is marvelous, and it is even more marvelous to think that *this hope came to us simply by hearing.* "Whereof ye heard before in the word of the truth of the gospel." "Faith cometh by hearing," and hope comes by faith; and so the divine hope of being in heaven came to us by hearing—not by working, not by deserving, not by penance and sacrifice, but simply by hearkening diligently unto the divine word and believing unto life. We heard that the pierced hand of Jesus had opened the kingdom of heaven to all believers, and we believed and saw a way of entrance into the holiest by His blood. We heard that God had prepared for them that love Him joys indescribable, and we believed the message, trusting in His Son.

Our confidence is in the word which we have heard, for it is written, "Hear and your soul shall live." We find that by hearing our confidence is strengthened, and our heart filled with inward assurance and joyful expectation, therefore do we love the word more and more. Will we not prize to the uttermost that sacred word which has brought us such a hope? Yes, that we will; till we exchange hearing for seeing and the message of Jesus for Jesus Himself, we will always lend a willing ear to the testimony of Jesus.

This hope is marvelous, once more, because *the substance of it is most extraordinary.* Beloved, what is the hope which is laid up for us in heaven? It would need many a sermon to bring out all the phases of delight which belong to that hope. It is the hope of *victory* for we shall overcome every foe, and Satan shall be trodden under our feet. A palm of victory is prepared for our hands, and a crown for our heads. Our life struggle shall not end in defeat but in complete and eternal triumph, for we shall overcome through the blood of the Lamb. Nor do we hope for victory only, but in our own persons we shall possess perfection. We shall one day cast off the slough of sin and shall be seen in the beauty of our newborn life. Truly "it doth not yet appear what we shall be," but when we think of the matchless character of our Lord Jesus, we are overjoyed by the assurance that "we shall be like him."

What an honor and a bliss for the younger brethren to be like the first born! To what higher honor could God Himself exalt us? I know not of aught which could surpass this. Oh matchless joy to be as holy, harmless, and undefiled as our own beloved Lord! How delightful to have no propensity to sin remaining in us nor trace of its ever having been there; how blissful to perceive that our holy desires and aspirations have no weakness or defect remaining in them.

Our nature will be perfect and fully developed in all its sinless excellence. We shall love God as we do now, but oh how much more intensely! We shall rejoice in God as we do now, but oh what depth there will be in that joy! We shall delight to serve Him as we do now, but there will then be no coldness of heart, no languor of spirit, no temptation to turn aside. Our service will be as perfect as that of angels. Then shall we say to ourselves without fear of any inward failure, "Bless the Lord, O my soul, and all that is within me bless his holy name." There will be no recreant affection then, no erring judgment, no straying passion, no rebellious lust. There will remain nothing which can defile or weaken or distract.

We shall be perfect, altogether perfect. This is our hope—victory over evil and perfection in all that is good. If this were all our hope it would be marvelous, but there is more to be unfolded.

We expect to enjoy security also from every danger. As there will be no evil in us, so there will be none around us or about us to cause us alarm. No temporal evil such as pain, bereavement, sorrow, labor, or reproach shall come near us. All will be security, peace, rest, and enjoyment. No mental evil will intrude upon us in heaven; no doubts, no staggering difficulties, no fears, no bewilderments will cause us distress. Here we see through a glass darkly, and we know in part, but then shall we see face to face and know even as we are known. Oh, to be free from mental trouble! What a relief will this be to many a doubting Thomas! This is a marvelous hope. And then no spiritual enemy will assail us; no world, no flesh, no devil will mar our rest above.

What will you make out of it, you tried ones? Your Sabbaths are very sweet now on earth, but when they are over you have to return to your cold world again. But there your Sabbath shall never end, and your separation from the wicked will be complete. It will be a strange sensation for you to find no Monday morning, no care to be renewed, no toil to be encountered, no harness to be buckled on afresh, and above all—no sin to be dreaded, no temptation to be escaped. Heaven is so peaceful that the storms of earth are there unknown, the stirrings of the flesh are never felt, and the howlings of the dog of hell are never heard. There all is peace and purity, perfection and security forever.

With this security will come perfect *rest*: "Yea, saith the Spirit, for they rest from their labors." Heavenly rest is quite consistent with *continual service*, for like the angels, we shall rest on the wing and find it rest to serve God day and night. But there you shall not toil till the sweat bedews your face, neither shall the sun smite you nor any heat. No weary limb nor fevered brain shall follow upon the blessed service of the glory-land. It is a paradise of pleasure and a palace of glory; it is a garden of supreme delights and a mansion of abiding love; it is an everlasting *sabbatismos*, a rest which never can be broken, which evermore remains for the people of God; it is a kingdom where all are kings, an inheritance where all are heirs. My soul longs for it. Is not this a charming hope? Did I not say well when I declared it to be marvelous?

Nor is this all, beloved, for we expect to enjoy in heaven a *happiness* beyond compare. Eye has not seen it nor ear heard it nor has the heart conceived it; it surpasses all carnal joy. We know a little of it, for the Lord has revealed it unto us by the Spirit who searches all things, even the deep things of God. Yet what we know is but a mere taste of the marriage feast—enough to make us long for more but by no means sufficient to give us a complete idea of the whole banquet. If it is so sweet to preach about Christ, what must it be to see Him and be with Him? If it is so delightful to be ravished by the music of His name, what must it be to lie in His bosom? Why, if these few grapes of Eshcol which are now and then brought to us are so sweet, what will it be to abide in the vineyard where all the clusters grow? If that one bucketful from the well of Bethlehem tasted so sweetly that we scarce dared to drink it but poured it out before the Lord as a thank offering, what a joy will it be to drink at the well-head without stint forever? O to be eternally at the right hand of God where there are pleasures forevermore!

This is our hope, and yet there is more, for we have the hope of everlasting *fellowship* with Christ. I would give ten thousand worlds, if I had them, to have one glimpse of that dear face which was marred with sorrow for my sake. But to sit at my Lord's feet and look up into His countenance and hear His voice and never, never grieve Him but to participate in all His triumphs and glories forever and forever—what a heaven will this be? Then shall we have fellowship with all His saints in whom He is glorified and by whom His image is reflected, and thus shall we behold fresh displays of His power and beamings of His love.

Is not this surpassing bliss? Said I not well when I declared that ours is a marvelous hope? Had I eloquence and could pile on goodly words and could a poet assist me with his sweetest song to tell of the bliss and joy of the eternal world, yet must preacher and poet both confess their inability to describe the glory to be revealed in us. The noblest intellect and the sweetest speech could not convey to you so much as a thousandth part of the bliss of heaven. There I leave the first head. It is a very marvelous hope.

A Secure Hope

Secondly, let us remark that IT IS A MOST SECURE HOPE. It is so according to the text, because *it is laid up* or secured. The recent calamities which have occurred in connection with the Glasgow City Bank will make business men very careful where they lay up their treasures, but no one can entertain any fear of the safety of that which God Himself takes under His charge. If your hope is laid up with Him, it becomes sinful to doubt its security. It is "laid up," the text says, and this means that it is hidden in a safe place like a treasure which is well secured. We find it hard to lay up our valuables safely in this world because thieves break through and steal; the iron safe, the strong room, and all sorts of inventions are employed to preserve them from felonious grip. But when God becomes the guardian of our treasure, He lays it up where none can touch it and neither man nor devil can steal it.

Our hope is laid up just as crowns and wreaths were laid up at the Grecian games for those who gained them. No one could snatch them away from their rightful owners, but the rewards were safely retained for the winners, to be distributed when the contest was over. You see not as yet your hope, beloved, but it is laid up. It is hidden with Christ in God and made as safe as the throne of God Himself.

Notice the next word, it is laid up *"for you."* It is something to have your hope laid up, but it is much better to have it laid up for yourself. "Laid up *for you*"; that is, for you whose faith is in Christ Jesus and who have love to all the saints. There is a crown in heaven which will never be worn by any head but yours; there is a harp in glory that never will be touched by any finger but yours. Make no mistake about it; it is laid up in heaven *for you*, "reserved in heaven *for you*, who are kept by the power of God, through faith unto salvation." "For *you*"—"Fear not, little flock; for it is your Father's good pleasure to give *you* the kingdom." Lay the stress there, and get honey out of it. "Laid up for *you*."

Where is it laid up? The next word tells us. "Laid up for you *in heaven*," "where," says the Savior as though He were expounding the text, "neither moth nor rust doth corrupt." This means that no process of decay will cause your treasure to become stale and worn out; no secret moth will eat the garments of heaven's courtiers, and no rust will tarnish the brightness of their crowns. Our Lord adds, "Nor do thieves break through nor steal." We cannot imagine a burglar's breaking through the walls of heaven. We could not imagine Satan himself undermining the bastions of the New Jerusalem or leaping over the bulwarks which guard the city of the Great King.

If your hope is laid up in heaven, it must be perfectly safe. If your hope lies in the bank, it may break; if it lies in an empire, it may melt away; if it lies in an estate, the title-deeds may be questioned; if it lies in any human creature, death may bereave you; if it lies in yourself, it is deceitful altogether. But if your hope is laid up in heaven, how secure it is. Be glad and bless the Lord.

To show how secure is our hope, the apostle tells us that we have an indisputable certificate and guarantee for it. He says, "We heard of it in the word of the truth of the gospel." Notice these three emphatic words—"In *the word* of *the truth* of *the gospel*." First, "In the word."

What word is that? Man's word? Man's words are so much wind. But this is God's Word, the same word that made heaven and earth, a word of power which cannot fail and of truth which cannot lie. You first hear of this blessed hope through the Word of God, and that Word is the best of evidence. You know how a person will say, "My word for it"—here you have God's Word for it. We take a good man's word freely, and will we not take God's Word much more readily? You have the Word of God for the sure hope that believers in Christ Jesus shall be blessed forever. Is not this security enough?

Our text goes on to say, "the word *of the truth*"; so then, it is not a word of guess, conjecture, or of probable inference, but of infallible truth. My brethren of the modern school, my wise brethren, have a word of excogitation and outcome and development, but the word the apostle preached was "the word of *the truth*"—something positive, dogmatic, and certain. Ugly as the word may sound, the Lord grant that we may never be ashamed of the thing *called* dogmatism nowadays which is none other than faith in God's truth.

We believe the Word of God not only to be true but to be "the word of *the* truth." "Let God be true and every man a liar." There may be other true things in the world, but God's Word is the essence of truth, *the* truth beyond all things else that may be true, for He has said, "Heaven and earth shall pass away, but my word shall never pass away." The apostle saith in another place, "All flesh is as glass, and all the glory of man as the flower of grass. The grass withereth, and the flower thereof falleth away; but the word of the Lord endureth forever. And this is the word which by the gospel is preached unto you."

Note the next word, "The word of the truth of *the gospel*," or of the good news. That is to say, the sum and substance of the good news is to be found in this glorious hope. If you extract the essence of the gospel and get *the* truth which is the central germ of the glad tidings, you come at that blessed hope most sure and steadfast which endures into that within the veil.

Now then, before your God-created hope can fail, the Word of God will have to be broken, but the Word of God cannot be broken. The truth will have to fail, but the truth abides forever and is by force of its own nature eternal, and the gospel will have to be disproved but that cannot be since the glory of God is made to hang upon it. You have heard it then, "in the word of the truth of the gospel," what better assurance do you need? Hold to it and rejoice in it, and you shall never be ashamed of your hope.

A Powerful Influence

I close by saying that IT IS A MOST POWERFULLY INFLUENTIAL HOPE. Brethren, I have already said to you that this hope is *the parent and nurse of love* because the text says, "The love which ye have to all the saints or the hope which is laid up for you in heaven." Now that is no trifling fountain of action which leads believing hearts to love, since love is always a working grace. Oh, for more love in this distracted world. Whatsoever in this world promotes Christian love is to be admired, and since the hope that we shall be forever together before the throne of God lifts us above the little disagreements of society and makes us affectionate to each other, it is a thing to cultivate with care.

Love is one part of the powerful operation of hope upon ourselves, but hopefulness affects others also. Where the hopefulness of saints is conspicuous, it leads ministers and gracious people to give thanks to God. Paul says, "We give thanks to God and the Father, praying always for you since we heard of your hope." I do not know a greater delight that a minister can have than the thought of all his people entering the bliss of heaven and of his meeting them all there.

We hardly have time to know each other here below; we have loved each other in the Lord, and we have striven together in the service of God, and some of us are old fellow-soldiers now after many years of Christian warfare. How pleasant it will be to dwell together above, world without end! Some have gone home whom we dearly loved and would almost have detained if we could, and there are others among us who in the order of nature will soon be translated; happy are we because we cannot long be separated.

The age of some among us prophesies their speedy departure and foreshadows that they will soon go over to the majority. But it is a most blessed reflection that all of us who are in Christ shall meet together above. We shall have ample room and verge enough for fellowship when we have reached eternity, and what will our joy be then!

Perhaps some of you will say to me when we converse in heavenly language—"You remember talking to us concerning the blessed hope on that fine Lord's day morning, but you did not know much about it. We said then, 'The half has not been told us', but now we perceive you did not tell us the one-hundredth part. Still we were glad to share in the joy of what little we did know and in the blessed hope of knowing so much more." O yes, dear friends, because the hope of heaven in us helps to make other people thank God on our account, it is a sweet grace and mightily influential, and the more we have of it the better.

Moreover, hearing of their hope *led the apostle to pray*, and if you will follow me in reading the words which succeed the text, you will see what he desired for his friends at Colosse. In the ninth verse you will see what he prayed for. He says, "For this cause we also, since the day we heard it, do not cease to pray for you and to desire that ye might be filled with the knowledge of his will in all wisdom and spiritual understanding." Having believed in Jesus and loving His people, you are going to heaven. So Paul says, "I desire that you be filled with the knowledge of his will," and well may he so desire, since to do that will is the joy and business of heaven. Is not our prayer, "Thy will be done on earth as it is in heaven"?

Beloved, let us learn the will of the Lord now and so be educated for the skies. Here we are to go through our apprenticeship that we may be able to take up our freedom as citizens of the New Jerusalem. Here we are at school, preparing to take our degree above among the instructed saints of God. Are we to enter heaven ignorant of what the will of the Lord is? Surely we ought to know something of the ways of the place, something of the rules of the court. This part of our life below is intended to be a prelude to our life above, a preparation for perfection.

Here below we undergo the tuning of the instruments. It is not meet that there should be discordant scrapings and screwings of strings in heaven. No, let us do all that here. Let us have our harps tuned below so that when we reach the orchestra of the skies, we may take our right place and drop into the right note directly. A good hope should make you eager to know the will of the Lord. It should purify you even as Christ is pure and make you anxious to begin the perfect service of heaven while yet you linger below.

Then the apostle prays "that ye might walk worthy of the Lord unto all pleasing." Is it not fit that you who are to rise to Enoch's heaven should walk as he did and have this testimony that you please God? You are going to dwell at God's right hand where there are pleasures forevermore, would not you wish to do all you can to please your Lord before you see Him? You are a son of a king. You have not put on your glittering array as yet; your crown is not yet on your head, but surely you wish to behave yourself as becomes one who is foreordained for so much honor and glory. If a son is in a distant country and is coming home, he begins to think "What can I take home? What can I do to please the beloved father whom I am soon to see?" Begin, beloved, to see what you can do to please God, because you are so soon to enter into His pleasure and dwell with those that wear white robes, "for they are worthy."

Next he says, "Being fruitful in every good work." Why, if there is to be such a rich reward of grace, let us bear all the gracious fruit we can, and if the time of working is so soon to be over, let us be instant in every holy labor while yet the season is with us. Who wants to go into heaven empty-handed? Who wishes to spend the time of his sojourning here in idleness? O no, let us seek to be fruitful to the glory of God that so we may have an abundant entrance into the kingdom.

The apostle further adds, "Increasing in the knowledge of God." If I am going to dwell with God, let me know somewhat of Him; let me search His Word and see how He has revealed himself; let me endeavor to have fellowship with Him and His Son Jesus that I may know Him. How can I enter heaven as a total stranger to Him who is the King of it? Is not the knowledge of God as needful as it is desirable? Those who have a good hope of heaven will not rest without knowing the Lord, from the least even to the greatest of them.

If anyone were to make you a present of a great estate, no matter in what country it might be situated, you would feel an interest in the land and its neighborhood, and before nightfall you would be found inquiring about the place. No matter how rustic the neighborhood or remote the locality, you would set your thoughts toward it if you knew the estate to be yours.

As a usual thing, one of the driest documents in all the world is a rich man's will. If you have ever heard one read, you will know how it proses on and on in that rigmarole fashion dear to lawyers. But if you are present when it is read to the family, please notice how "my son

John's" eyes clear up when it comes to the clause which concerns himself and how even the aged countenance of "my faithful servant Jane" brightens when her small legacy is mentioned.

Everyone is on the alert when his own interests are affected. Even so he that has a hope in heaven and an interest in Christ's great testament will at once take an interest in divine things and will desire to increase in the knowledge of God.

Once again the apostle says, "strengthened with all might, according to His glorious power, unto all patience and long-suffering with joyfulness." A hope of heaven is a mighty strengthener for bearing the ills of life and the persecutions of the adversary. "It will soon be over," says a man who looks for heaven, and therefore he is not overweighted with grief. "It is an ill lodging," said the traveler, "but I shall be away in the morning." Well may we be strengthened with all might by the hope of heaven. It is but reason that the exceeding weight of glory should cast into the shade this light affliction which is but for a moment.

You will say, "But have you not wrought this part of the chapter into your subject without any warrant?" No. Here is my warrant in the next verse: "Giving thanks unto the Father, which has made us meet to be partakers of the inheritance of the saints in light." I have been following the evident track of the apostle's thoughts: The Lord gives us a hope of glory, and then He gives us a meetness for it, and that meetness is largely wrought in us by the Holy Spirit through the instrumentality of our hope.

Cultivate, then, your hope, dearly beloved. Make it to shine so plainly in you that your minister may hear of your hopefulness and joy; cause observers to take note of it because you speak of heaven and act as though you really expected to go there. Make the world know that you have a hope of heaven. Make worldlings feel that you are a believer in eternal glory and that you hope to be where Jesus is. Often surprise them as they see what they call your simplicity, but what is in truth only your sincerity, while you treat as matter of fact the hope laid up for you in heaven. The Lord grant it for Jesus Christ's sake. Amen.

Apostolic Optimism

John Henry Jowett (1864–1923) was known as "the greatest preacher in the English-speaking world." Born in Yorkshire, England, he was ordained into the Congregational ministry. His second pastorate was at the famous Carr's Lane Church, Birmingham, where he followed the eminent Dr. Robert W. Dale. From 1911–18, he pastored the Fifth Avenue Presbyterian Church, New York City, and from 1918–23, he ministered at Westminster Chapel, London, succeeding G. Campbell Morgan. He wrote many books of devotional messages and sermons.

This message is from *Apostolic Optimism*, published by Richard R. Smith, Inc., New York, in 1930.

John Henry Jowett

11

APOSTOLIC OPTIMISM

Rejoicing in hope (Romans 12:12).

THAT IS A characteristic expression of the fine, genial optimism of the Apostle Paul. His eyes are always illumined. The cheery tone is never absent from his speech. The buoyant and springy movement of his life is never changed. The light never dies out of his sky. Even the gray firmament reveals more hopeful tints and becomes significant of evolving glory. The apostle is an optimist, "rejoicing in hope," a child of light wearing the "armor of light," "walking in the light" even as Christ is in the light.

This apostolic optimism was not a thin and fleeting sentiment begotten of a cloudless summer day. It was not the creation of a season; it was the permanent pose of the spirit. Even when beset with circumstances which to the world would spell defeat, the apostle moved with the mien of a conqueror. He never lost the kingly posture. He was disturbed by no timidity about ultimate issues. He fought and labored in the spirit of certain triumph. "We are always confident." "We are more than conquerors through Him that loved us." "Thanks be unto God who giveth us the victory through our Lord Jesus Christ."

This apostolic optimism was not born of sluggish thinking or of idle and shallow observation. I am very grateful that the counsel of my text lifts its chaste and cheery flame in the 12th chapter of an epistle of which the first chapter contains as dark and searching an indictment of our nature as the mind of man has ever drawn. Let me rehearse the appalling catalogue that the radiance of the apostle's optimism may appear the more abounding: "Senseless hearts," "fools," "uncleanness," "vile" "reprobate minds," "unrighteousness, wickedness, covetousness, maliciousness; full of envy, murder, strife, deceit, malignity, whisperers, backbiters, hateful to God, insolent, haughty, boastful, inventors of evil things, without understanding, covenant-breakers, without natural affection, unmerciful."

With fearless severity the apostle leads us through the black realms of midnight and eclipse. And yet in the subsequent reaches of the great argument of which these dark regions form the preface, there emerges the clear, calm, steady light of my optimistic text. I say it is not the buoyancy of ignorance. It is not the flippant, light-hearted expectancy of a man who knows nothing about the secret places of the night. The counselor is a man who has steadily gazed at light at its worst, who has dug through the outer walls of convention and respectability, who has pushed his way into the secret chambers and closets of the life, who has dragged out the slimy sins which were lurking in their holes and named them after their kind. It is this man who when he has surveyed the dimensions of evil and misery and contempt merges his dark indictment in a cheery and expansive dawn, in an optimistic evangel, in which he counsels his fellow disciples to maintain the confident attitude of a rejoicing hope.

The Secrets of Optimism

Now what are the secrets of this courageous and energetic optimism? Perhaps if we explore the life of this great apostle and seek to discover its springs, we may find the clue to his abounding hope. Roaming then through the entire records of his life and teachings, do we discover any significant emphasis? Preeminent above all other suggestions, I am impressed with his vivid sense of the reality of the redemptive work of Christ. Turn where I will, the redemptive work of the Christ evidences itself as the base and groundwork of his life. It is not only that here and there are solid statements of doctrine wherein some massive argument is constructed for the partial unveiling of redemptive glory.

Even in those parts of his epistles where formal argument has ceased and where solid doctrine is absent, the doctrine flows as a fluid element into the practical convictions of life and determines the shape and quality of the judgments. Nay, one might legitimately use the figure of a finer medium still and say that in all the spacious reaches of the apostle's life, the redemptive work of his Master is present as an atmosphere in which all his thoughts and purposes and labors find their sustaining and enriching breath.

Take this epistle to the Romans in which my text is found. The earlier stages of the great epistle are devoted to a massive and stately presentation of the doctrines of redemption. But when I turn over the pages where the majestic argument is concluded, I find the doctrine persisting in a diffused and rarefied form and appearing as the determining factor in the solution of practical problems. If he is dealing with the question of the "eating of meats," the great doctrine reappears and interposes its solemn and yet elevating principle: "destroy not him with thy meat for whom Christ died."

If he is called upon to administer rebuke to the passionate and unclean, the shadow of the Cross rests upon his judgment. "Ye are not your own; ye are bought with a price." If he is portraying the ideal relationship of husband and wife, he sets it in the light of redemptive glory: "Husbands, love your wives, even as Christ also loved the Church, and gave Himself up for it." If he is seeking to cultivate the grace of liberality, he brings the heavenly air round about the spirit. "Ye know the grace of our Lord Jesus Christ, that though He was rich, yet for your sakes He became poor." It interweaves itself with all his salutations. It exhales in all his benedictions like a hallowing fragrance. You cannot get away from it. In the light of the glory of redemption all relationships are assorted and arranged.

Redemption was not degraded into a fine abstract argument to which the apostle had appended his own approval and then with sober satisfaction had laid it aside as a practical irrelevancy in the stout chests of mental orthodoxy. It became the very spirit of his life. It was, if I may be allowed the violent figure, the warm blood in all his judgment. It filled the veins of all his thinking. It beat like a pulse in all his purposes. It determined and vitalized his decisions in the crisis as well as in the lesser trifles of the common day. His conception of redemption was regulative of all his thought.

But it is not only the immediacy of redemption in the apostle's thought by which I am impressed. I stand in awed amazement before its vast, far-stretching reaches into the eternities. Said an old villager to me concerning the air of his elevated hamlet, "Aye, sir, it's a fine air is this westerly breeze; I like to think of it as having traveled from the distant fields of the Atlantic!" And here is the Apostle Paul with the quickening wind of redemption blowing about him in loosening, vitalizing, strengthening influence. To him in all his thinking it had its birth in the distant fields of eternity!

To the apostle redemption was not a small device, an afterthought, a patched-up expedient to meet an unforeseen emergency. The redemptive purpose lay back in the abyss of the eternities, and in a spirit of reverent questioning the apostle sent his trembling thoughts into those lone and silent fields. He emerged with whispered secrets such as these: "fore-knew," "foreordained," "chosen in Him before the foundation of the world," "eternal life promised before times eternal," "the eternal purpose which He purposed in Christ Jesus our Lord."

Beloved, does our common thought of redemptive glory reach back into this august and awful presence? Does the thought of the modern disciple journey in this distant pilgrimage? Or do we now regard it as unpractical and irrelevant? There is no more insidious peril in modern religious life than the debasement of our conception of the practical. If we divorce the practical from the sublime, the practical will become the superficial and will degenerate into a very lean and forceless thing. When Paul went on this lonely pilgrimage, his spirit acquired the posture of a finely sensitive reverence.

People who live and move beneath great domes acquire a certain calm and stately dignity. It is in companionship with the sublimities that awkwardness and coarseness are destroyed. We lose our reverence when we desert the august. But has reverence no relationship to the practical? Shall we discard it as an irrelevant factor in the wealthy purposes of common life? Why, reverence is the very clue to fruitful, practical living. Reverence is creative of hope; nay, a more definite emphasis can be given to the assertion; reverence is a constituent of hope. Annihilate reverence and life loses its fine sensitiveness, and when sensitiveness goes out of a life, the hope that remains is only a flippant rashness, a thoughtless impetuosity, the careless onrush of the kine, and not a firm assured perception of a triumph that is only delayed.

A reverent homage before the sublimities of yesterday is the condition of a fine perception of the hidden triumphs of the morrow. And, therefore, I do not regard it as an accidental conjunction that the psalmist puts them together and proclaims the evangel that "the Lord taketh pleasure in them that *fear* Him, in them that *hope* in His mercy." To feel the days before me I must revere the purpose which throbs behind me. I must bow in reverence if I would anticipate in hope.

Here, then, is the Apostle Paul with the redemptive purpose interweaving itself with all the entanglements of his common life—a purpose reaching back into the awful depths of the eternities and issuing from those depths in amazing fullness of grace and glory. No one can be five minutes in the companionship of the Apostle Paul without discovering how wealthy is his sense of the wealthy, redeeming ministry of God. What a wonderful consciousness he has of the sweep and fullness of the divine grace! You know the variations of the glorious air: "the unsearchable riches of Christ"; "riches in glory in Christ Jesus"; "all spiritual blessings in the heavenly places in Christ"; "the riches of His goodness and forbearance and longsuffering."

The redemptive purpose of God bears upon the life of the apostle and upon the race whose privileges he shares, not in an uncertain and reluctant shower but in a great and marvelous flood. And what to him is the resultant enfranchisement? What are the spacious issues of the glorious work? Do you recall those wonderful sentences scattered here and there about the apostle's writings and beginning with the words "but now"? Each sentence proclaims the end of the dominion of night and unveils some glimpse of the new created day. "But now!" It is a phrase that heralds a great deliverance! "But now, apart from the law the righteousness of God hath been manifested."

"But now, being made free from sin and become servants to God." "But now in Christ Jesus ye that once were far off are made nigh in the blood of Christ." "But now are ye light in the Lord." "Now, no condemnation to them that are in Christ Jesus." These represent no thin abstractions. To Paul the realities of which they speak were more real than the firm and solid earth. And is it any wonder that a man with such a magnificent sense of the reality of the redemptive works of Christ, who felt the eternal purpose throbbing in the dark backward and abyss of time, who conceived it operating upon our race in floods of grace and glory, and who realized in his own immediate consciousness the varied wealth of the resultant emancipation—is it any wonder that for this man a new day had dawned, and the birds had begun to sing and the flowers to bloom, and a sunny optimism had taken possession of his heart which found expression in an assured and rejoicing hope?

The Resources for Optimism

I look abroad again over the record of this man's life and teachings, if perchance I may discover the secrets of his abiding optimism, and I am profoundly impressed by his living sense of the reality and greatness of his present resources. "By Christ redeemed!" Yes, but that is only the Alpha and not the Omega of the work of grace. "By Christ redeemed!" That is not a grand finale; it is only a glorious inauguration. "By Christ redeemed; in Christ restored"; it is with these dynamics of restoration that his epistles are so wondrously abounding. In almost every other sentence he suggests a dynamic which he can count upon as his friend.

Paul's mental and spiritual outlook comprehended a great army of positive forces laboring in the interests of the kingdom of God. His conception of life was amazingly rich in friendly dynamics! I do not wonder that such a wealthy consciousness was creative of a triumphant optimism.

Just glance at some of the apostle's auxiliaries: "Christ lives in me!" "Christ lives in me! He breathes through all my aspirations. He thinks through all my thinking. He wills through all my willing. He loves through all my loving. He travails in all my labors. He works within me 'to will and to do of His good pleasure.'" That is the primary faith of the hopeful life. But see what follows in swift and immediate succession. "If Christ is in you, the spirit is life." "The spirit is life!" And therefore you find that in the apostle's thought, dispositions are powers. They are not passive entities. They are positive forces vitalizing and energizing the common life of men.

Beloved, I am persuaded there is a perilous leakage in this department of our thought. We are not bold enough in our thinking concerning spiritual realities. We do not associate with every mode of the consecrated spirit the mighty energy of God. We too often oust from our practical calculations some of the strongest and most aggressive allies of the saintly life. Meekness is more than the absence of self-assertion; it is the manifestation of the mighty power of God.

To the Apostle Paul love expressed more than a relationship. It was an energy productive of abundant labors. Faith was more than an attitude. It was an energy creative of mighty endeavor. Hope was more than a posture. It was an energy generative of a most enduring patience. All these are dynamics to be counted as active allies cooperating in the ministry of the kingdom.

And so the epistles abound in the recital of mystic ministries at work. The Holy Spirit works! Grace works! Faith works! Love works! Hope works! Prayer works! And there are other allies robed in less attractive garb. "Tribulation works!" "This light affliction works." "Godly sorrow works!"

On every side of him the apostle conceives cooperative and friendly powers. "The mountain is full of horses and chariots of fire round about him." He exults in the consciousness of abounding resources. He discovers the friends of God in things which find no place among the scheduled powers of the world. He finds God's raw material in the world's discarded waste. "Weak things," "base things," "things that are despised," "things that are not," mere nothings; among these he discovers the operating agents of the mighty God. Is it any wonder that in this man, possessed of such a wealthy consciousness of multiplied resources, the spirit of a cheery optimism should be enthroned?

With what stout confidence he goes into the fight! He never mentions the enemy timidly. He never seeks to underestimate his strength. Nay, again and again he catalogues all possible antagonisms in a spirit of buoyant and exuberant triumph. However numerous the enemy, however subtle and aggressive his devices, however towering and well-established the iniquity, however black the gathering clouds, so sensitive is the apostle to the wealthy resources of God that amid it all he remains a sunny optimist, "rejoicing in hope," laboring in the spirit of a conqueror even when the world was exulting in his supposed discomfiture and defeat.

The Realities of Optimism

And, finally, in searching for the springs of this man's optimism, I place alongside his sense of the reality of redemption and his wealthy consciousness of present resources, his impressive sense of the reality of future glory. Paul gave himself time to think of heaven, of the home of God, of his own home when time should be no more. He loved to contemplate "the glory that shall be revealed." He mused in wistful expectancy of the day "when Christ who is our life shall be manifested," and when we also "shall be manifested with Him in glory." He pondered the thought of death as "gain," as transferring him to conditions in which he would be "at home with the Lord," "with Christ, which is far better." He looked for "the blessed hope and appearing of the glory of our great God and Savior Jesus Christ," and he contemplated "that great day" as the "henceforth" which would reveal to him the crown of righteousness and glory.

Is anyone prepared to dissociate this contemplation from

the apostle's cheery optimism? Is not rather the thought of coming glory one of its abiding springs? Can we safely exile it from our moral and spiritual culture? I know that this particular contemplation is largely absent from modern religious life, and I know the nature of the recoil in which our present impoverishment began. "Let us hear less about the mansions of the blest and more about the housing of the poor!"

Men revolted against an effeminate contemplation which had run to seed in favor of an active philanthropy which sought the enrichment of the common life. But beloved, pulling a plant up and throwing it upon the dung-heap is not the only way of saving it from running to seed. You can accomplish by a wise restriction what is wastefully done by severe destruction.

I think we have lost immeasurably by the uprooting in so many lives of this plant of heavenly contemplation. We have built on the erroneous assumption that the contemplation of future glory inevitably unfits us for the service of man. It is an egregious and destructive mistake.

I do not think that Richard Baxter's labors were thinned or impoverished by his contemplation of "the saints' everlasting rest." When I consider his mental output, his abundant labors as Father-confessor to a countless host, his pains and persecutions and imprisonments, I cannot but think he received some of the powers of his optimistic endurance from contemplations such as he counsels in his incomparable book. "Run familiarly through the streets of the heavenly Jerusalem; visit the patriarchs and prophets, salute the apostles, and admire the armies of martyrs; lead on the heart from street to street, bring it into the palace of the great King; lead it, as it were, from chamber to chamber. Say to it, 'Here must I lodge, here must I die, here must I praise, here must I love and be loved. My tears will then be wiped away, my groans be turned to another tune, my cottage of clay be changed to this palace, my prison rags to these splendid robes'; 'for the former things are passed away.'"

I cannot think that Samuel Rutherford impoverished his spirit or deadened his affections or diminished his labors by mental pilgrimages such as he counsels to Lady Cardoness: "Go up beforehand and see your lodging. Look through all your Father's rooms in Heaven. Men take a sight of the lands ere they buy them. I know that Christ hath made the bargain already; but be kind to the house ye are going to, and see it often." I cannot think that this would imperil the fruitful optimisms of the Christian life.

I often examine with peculiar interest the hymnbook we use at Carr's Lane. It was compiled by Dr. Dale. Nowhere else can I find the broad perspective of his theology and his primary help-meets in the devotional life as I find them there. And is it altogether unsuggestive that under the heading of "Heaven" is to be found one of the largest sections of the book? A greater space is given to "Heaven" than is given to "Christian duty." Is it not significant of what a great man of affairs found needful for the enkindling and sustenance of a courageous hope? And among the hymns are many which have helped to nourish the sunny endeavors of a countless host.

> There is a land of pure delight
> Where saints immortal reign;
> Infinite day excludes the night,
> And pleasures banish pain.
>
> What are these, arrayed in white,
> Brighter than the noonday sun?
> Foremost of the suns of light,
> Nearest the eternal throne.
>
> Hark! hark, my soul! Angelic songs are swelling
> O'er earth's green fields and ocean's wave-beat shore.
> Angelic songs to sinful men are telling
> Of that new life when sin shall be no more.

Beloved, depend upon it, we are not impoverished by contemplations such as these. They take no strength out of the hand, and they put much strength and buoyancy into the heart. I proclaim the contemplation of coming glory as one of the secrets of the apostle's optimism which enabled him to labor and endure in the confident spirit of rejoicing hope. These then are some of the springs of Christian optimism, some of the sources in which we may nourish our hope in the newer labors of a larger day: a sense of the glory of the past in a perfected redemption, a sense of the glory of the present in our multiplied resources, a sense of the glory of tomorrow in the fruitful rest of our eternal home.

> O, blessed hope! with this elate
> Let not our hearts be desolate;
> But, strong in faith and patience, wait
> Until He come!

Hope for Backsliders

Amzi Clarence Dixon (1854–1925) was a Baptist preacher who ministered to several congregations in the south before becoming pastor of the Moody Memorial Church in Chicago (1906–11). He left Chicago to pastor the famous Metropolitan Tabernacle in London, "Spurgeon's Tabernacle" (1911–19). He died in 1925 while pastoring the University Baptist Church, Baltimore, Maryland. A close associate of Reuben A. Torrey, Dixon helped him edit *The Fundamentals*. Dixon was a popular preacher in both Britain and America.

This message is from *Through Night to Morning*.

Amzi Clarence Dixon

12

HOPE FOR BACKSLIDERS

I will heal their backslidings (Hosea 14:4).

THE BOOK OF HOSEA is God's message to the backslider. Follow the name of Ephraim through the book, and you will see the experience of an impenitent backslider. He is—

1. GOD-FORSAKEN. "Ephraim is joined to idols, let him alone" (Hos. 5:3). What can God do for a man who will not confess and forsake his sin, except just let him alone? And to be let alone of God while sin works in us its direful results is a pitiable state.

2. DESOLATE. "Ephraim shall be desolate in the day of rebuke" (5:9). Without God the backslider's condition becomes desolate indeed, and loving rebuke which he resents increases the desolation.

3. OPPRESSED. "Ephraim is oppressed and broken in judgment" (5:14). Desolation becomes oppression. Emptiness becomes burden. The judgments of God, if they lead to repentance, will bless us. But if we resent them, they will break us. When we violate law, physical or moral, we do not break the law so much as it breaks us.

4. FALSE. "They commit falsehood" (7:1). "Ephraim compasseth me about with lies." The backslider's life is apt to be a living lie. He tries to appear happy when he is really miserable. He poses for a good man when he knows he is bad. Hypocrisy becomes a habit with him.

5. INCONSISTENT. "Ephraim is a cake not turned" (7:8). He is overdone on one side and underdone on the other. On the side of formal ritualistic observance he is apt to be overdone; on the side of genuine, solid Christian living he is underdone. The backslider often tries to make up for his lack of piety by excess of religious form. His songs and

responses on Sunday may be loud, while his living during the week is low. He "is a cake unturned," burnt on one side and raw on the other.

6. FOOLISH AND COWARDLY. "Ephraim is also like a silly dove without heart." The dove is a symbol of gentleness, and the backslider, though he may be gentle, is certain to be silly. He will talk and act foolishly. The language of Zion on his lips sounds silly; it lacks the ring of reality. His prayers are without heart, and when he is asked to do something for Christ, he is too cowardly to undertake it.

7. SELFISH. "Ephraim is an empty vine; he bringeth forth fruit unto himself" (10:1). Like the vine that bears no clusters of grapes for others but keeps all its life of root and branch simply to add to its own length and leaf, the backslider holds his own and builds up only himself. He seeks his own profit and pleasure. He uses his money in advancing his own interest. He begins to talk against foreign missions, because he cannot see the good of sending men and money to the heathen while there is so much need at home. He is afraid that somebody will get something out of him. He hates collections, because they bring nothing to him but are an attempt to gather fruit from the empty vine of his stingy soul. Not what can I give, but what can I get? is the question he asks of everything he sees. He begins to be a Dead Sea taking in a Jordan of blessing and holding it without an outlet. The result is emptiness, for not a living thing thrives in the waters of his selfish life.

8. UNSATISFIED. "Ephraim feedeth on wind, and followeth after the east wind" (12:1). The backslider misuses the gifts of God. Wind is good as breath but bad as food. If he would breathe it, he would be invigorated, but his eating it fills him with emptiness and distress. So the gifts of God received gratefully and used rightly will bless and satisfy us, but received without gratitude and used only upon self, they do not satisfy the soul. And the backslider turns from the solid food of God's Word to the wind of light literature, from the satisfying manna of truth to the east wind of fiction. He ceases to relish the table of the

Lord spread Sunday after Sunday in the sanctuary, while he feeds upon the wind of the theater during the week. He neglects the strengthening meat of God's service and runs after the east wind of the dance and the card party. If he is not poisoned by the malaria in it, he soon becomes a weak, emaciated invalid, because his soul has been starved by the lack of nourishment. He is a spiritual suicide.

9. VAINGLORIOUS. "When Ephraim spake trembling, he exalted himself" (13:1). The backslider has lost the steady accent of faith. His voice trembles with fear. He begins to doubt everything and everybody. The sound of the wind upon which he feeds frightens him. He is restless at church, at the theater and dance. He fits nowhere. But he must brace up and assert himself. He becomes self-conscious and soon swells with vanity. He magnifies the self-element in religion. His motto is "that if a man does not esteem himself very highly, no one else will esteem him." The trembling doubter has developed into a boastful Pharisee. He quits praying, for "Why should a man of so much importance be all the time begging God to help him? God helps those who help themselves." The inflation of self has at last well nigh excluded God from his life. The knowledge that puffs up has banished the love that builds up. He has become a walking, talking capital I.

For such a backslider there is no hope so long as he is impenitent, but hope dawns the moment he returns to God and confesses his sin. "O, Israel, return unto the Lord thy God, for thou hast fallen by thy iniquity. Say, take away all our iniquity, and receive us graciously." After such a full confession without excuse or palliation, God begins to deal with His penitent child in the most gracious and tender manner—

1. HE HEALS. "I will heal their backsliding." There are two kinds of healing. One has to do with wounds, the other with disease. Some soldiers on campaign need the healing of wounds; others of disease; and still others, sick and wounded, need both kinds of healing. Sin treats some as the robbers on the way from Jerusalem to Jericho

treated the traveler. It cuts and bruises, leaving them half dead. They are surprised, overtaken in a fault. Almost before they know it, they were attacked and hurt.

They need the treatment of the good Samaritan who took the wounded man in hand and cared for him until his wounds were healed. With other backsliders sin is a deep-seated disease and needs constitutional treatment. Blessed fact it is that Jesus Christ is surgeon for the wounded, and physician for the diseased. His blood is equally good for wound and disease. We need not stop to discuss the different methods of treatment. The fact that healing is possible is the thing which interests us now, and we can safely leave the methods to the physician into whose hands we have placed our case.

2. HE LOVES. "I will love them freely." The word "freely" means that He loves of Himself, not because He sees traits of character that call forth His love, but just because He cannot help it. It is His nature. The backslider is apt to be discouraged by the thought that God does not love him, because by his sins he has made himself so unlovely.

It is true that a backslider is an unlovely character; but, take heart, God does not love you because you are lovely, but because He is loving. The spring of love is not in you but in Himself. He is a fountain of love, and fountains, you know, do not have to be induced to flow. The water is sent forth by an inner force. When the water must be drawn, it has ceased to be a fountain. Backsliding brother, bring the empty vessel of your penitent soul beneath the overflowing fountain of God's infinite love and be filled with His fullness.

3. HE DRAWS NEAR. "I will be as the dew unto Israel." The dew does its work by gentle contact, and it is quiet in its working. There is no sound of saw or hammer. God is as the lion against those who refuse to repent. He is as the dew unto every penitent soul, reviving weak and struggling life. "But," says the backslider, "I am in the dark, I have no comfort." Yes, but remember, the dew does its work in the dark. It distills in the night. In the night of your penitent grief let God deal with you in

gentleness and love. This gentle dealing in the dark will prepare you for His coming as the morning when your soul will be filled with the light of the sun of righteousness.

4. HE GIVES GROWTH. "He shall grow as the lily." The lily grows rapidly. And when a backslider has truly repented, he may grow in grace with great rapidity. While living in sin, he has not grown a particle. He has been stunted and withered. But with a consciousness of being healed and loved freely and now enveloped in God's care as the plant is enveloped in the refreshing dew, he cannot help growing like the lily.

5. HE GIVES STABILITY. "He shall cast forth his roots like Lebanon." The lily is frail. You can break it or uproot it with your finger. But not so with the cedar of Lebanon. Its roots go deep into the earth and wrap themselves around the rocks. It can stand in the face of the storm and defy its fury.

So the penitent backslider, while he grows rapidly like the lily, will become stable like the cedar. He fell because he lacked stability, but his sad experience has taught him not to rely at all upon his own strength while he leans with all his weight upon the strength of God. Peter, by his unhappy fall at the trial of Christ, was cured of all boasting; he never fell again. He has now become truly a rock in his resistance of evil. David's fall was shameful, but his recovery was complete, and he never fell again. He grew like the lily and was as strong as a cedar in Lebanon.

6. HE MAKES HIM BEAUTIFUL. "His beauty shall be as the olive tree." The beauty of the lily is in its delicate texture and coloring. A touch or blot will mar it, and once marred it can never be restored. The backslider need not expect to recover the virgin beauty of the lily which he had before sin blunted and bruised him. The scars of sin will remain even after the wound has been healed.

The olive tree, on the other hand, may not be in itself beautiful. It is often gnarled and crooked. Its beauty is chiefly in its fruitfulness. When the tree is full of olives, you forget the unsightliness of its trunk and branches while you gaze at the beauty of its fruit. So the penitent backslider, while he mourns the loss of the lily's beauty, may rejoice in the beauty of the olive's fruitfulness.

As Peter thought of his shameful backsliding, he doubtless strove to be more fruitful. He may have preached better at Pentecost as he thought of his swearing at the trial of Jesus, because he wished to make amends for the harm he had done. David, after his brokenhearted penitence, bore the fruit of the fifty-first Psalm. May God help us to make up for the loss of lily beauty by the beauty of olive fruitfulness.